DATE DUE		
MAY 2 2 1989		
NOV 0 3 1997		
APR 1 5 1998		

Government and Politics in Islam

To Shereen and Jenann,
our first projects together

Government and Politics in Islam

Tareq Y. Ismael and Jacqueline S. Ismael

ST. MARTIN'S PRESS, New York

Printed in Great Britain
First published in the United States of America in 1985

Library of Congress Cataloging in Publication Data

Ismael, Tareq Y.
    Government and politics in Islam.
    Bibliography: P.
    Includes index.
    1. Islam and politics—Near East.   2. Near East—
Politics and government—1945–   I. Ismael,
Jacqueline S.   II. Title.
BP63.A4N42438   1985   320.5′5′0917671   85–2263

ISBN 0–312–34126–1

Contents

List of Figures

Preface

Since the early 1970s, the Islamic world has been experiencing a phenomenon to which different names – Islamic revival, Islamic awakening, Islamic tide, Islamic resurgence – have been attributed. Despite the different terminology, these names all refer to the emergence of politically active Islamic groups that oppose the political regimes, in their present forms, in all Islamic countries, and that call for a return to the original principles of the Islamic state.

The fact that such a phenomenon clearly manifested itself in the Islamic world, starting in the early 1970s, does not mean that it did not exist before that period. Actually, Islamic history has witnessed numerous activist movements, in both intellectual and practical form. In the early 1970s, this activist phenomenon began making itself felt in fundamental ways within local and regional politics. It assumed an international dimension with the success of the Islamic revolution in Iran and the fall of the Shah's regime in 1979.

Following the outbreak of the Iranian revolution, the Islamic phenomenon became a major issue of concern – especially in the West – at all levels. On the academic level, much research and analysis was undertaken to study and examine the phenomenon. On the official level, both the West and the Islamic world showed special interest and concern, particularly after Iranian militant students were able to hold hostage members of the American embassy in Tehran, and after declarations by the leaders of the new Iranian regime that they intended to export their revolution to neighbouring countries. In addition to the Iranian revolution, the occupation of the 'Kaaba' in Saudi Arabia by a religious group led by Juhaiman al-Utaibi in 1979, and the assassination of President Anwar al-Sadat of Egypt in 1981, caused more concern about the Islamic phenomenon at official levels in the West and the Islamic world.

This study examines Islamic political activism from two dimensions: historically, in Part I (The Intellectual Foundation), from the perspective of the intellectual foundations of political thought in Islam; contemporarily, in Part II (Modern Activism), from the perspective of case studies of the phenomenon. Chapters 1 and 2 investigate the intellectual foundations of classical and modern Islamic political thought; Chapter 3 investigates the Muslim Brotherhood as a prototype of contemporary Islamic political activism. Chapters 4 and 5 examine Islamic activism in Iran and Egypt – the two primary cases in the region, from an international perspective. Chapter 6 provides a survey of popular Islamic activism in other countries of the Middle East and North Africa, an overview of official Islamic activism, and a consideration of the major characteristics of the movement derived from the cases examined. Finally, the appendices are provided to illustrate the utilization of Islamic religious symbolism by heads of state anxious to justify the existing political, social and economic order.

The study relies heavily upon primary and secondary Arabic sources. In transliterating names, titles, etc., a phonetic rather than linguistic system of transliteration has been used.

We wish to acknowledge with appreciation the research assistance of Rex Brynen and his direct collaboration in the preparation of Chapter 5; also, Alex Brynen, who provided some research assistance and helped edit the manuscript. We are indebted to Professor Ali E.H. Dessouki of Cairo University for his careful examination of Chapter 5. Finally, Mary Gray and Judi Powell typed many drafts and redrafts of each chapter. Their patience and good humour are well beyond the call of duty and deserve special commendation.

Calgary, Alberta
January 1985

PART I

The Intellectual Foundations

1 Classic Islamic Political Thought

Islamic political thought reflects some fourteen centuries of Islamic philosophic and theoretical inquiry into the nature and role of government, its relationship to religious and temporal affairs, and its relationship to social change and social revolution within the Islamic world and beyond. The analysis of this theoretical and intellectual basis of Islamic government and society has been given only scant attention by Western scholars in understanding the forces of change impacting on contemporary Islamic societies. Indeed, Islam has usually been perceived as a 'traditional' force, resisting progressive change and consequently constituting a negative influence or barrier to social and political development. This image of Islam as a static rather than dynamic system of thought has contributed to the failure to recognize the significance of Islamic solutions to the issues of social and political development.

The separation of state and religion in modern Western societies produced a clear separation between the realms of religious and temporal affairs. While spiritual and ethical issues became the domain of philosophy and theology, temporal issues became the domain of political and sociological theory. In this framework, religious and social thought developed autonomously of each other, and the issues of social and political change were rendered distinct from the issues of spiritual and ethical development.

However, in a religiously-based socio-political system, this separation does not exist. According to an eminent scholar of Islam:

> The discussion in Islamic political thought on 'divine rights' means the 'right of the society' . . . and the discussion on 'God's jurisdiction and domain' actually means, in political terms, 'the jurisdiction of the nation and its domain . . . .' There is no contradiction here in the fact that the domain belongs to God but the political jurisdiction and Government in Islamic society lay in the hands of the Moslem people.[1]

3

With no distinct separation between the profound and the profane, political and social issues must be addressed within the framework of religious ideology; and political and social conflicts must be manifested in spiritual and ethical contention. As a socio-political religious system, Islam incorporated both temporal and spiritual affairs. The natures of the political state and the spiritual state, of political legitimacy and religious legitimacy, of ideology and doctrine, are not conceptualized and analysed distinctly, but are highly interrelated in Islamic thought. Thus, the development of Islamic thought reflected and reflected upon the dynamic of social change that catalysed it. This interrelationship between the temporal and the spiritual was first manifested in the problem of succession.

Succession: Political Legitimacy in Islam

The position of the Prophet Muhammad in the early Muslim community as God's appointed religious and temporal representative was a central factor in keeping the Muslim community (*umma*) united politically and religiously. The accepted infallibility of the Prophet's authority in all matters gave the community a unified outlook on life, religion, and politics. His death in AD 632 (the eleventh year of hijra), however, forced the Muslims to begin to look for answers to the immediate tasks that suddenly faced them. How should they govern themselves? Who would be the successor? What kind of a government should they have? What would be the 'Islamic' method of choosing a successor to the Prophet? Who would be best qualified to run the affairs of the community?

The only traditions the new Muslim community had to draw upon in choosing a successor to the Prophet were pre-Islamic, tribal customs. However, the community transcended the tribe in terms of membership, uniting members across tribal lines and superseding tribal bonds and loyalties with community bonds and loyalties. Nevertheless, tribal identities and tribal patterns, especially inter-tribal rivalries, were a source of tensions that became manifest immediately upon the Prophet's death since there was no clear successor and each tribal group attempted to establish a prior claim on the position.

The Muslims of Medina (the 'Ansar', or the Prophet's Partisans) held a meeting in their tribal community hall in Medina at Saqifat Bani Sa'eda to choose a successor to the Prophet even before the Prophet's body was buried, as was customary among pre-Islamic Arabian tribes when selecting a new head (*sheikh*). They saw themselves as the legitimate successors since they had come to the aid of the Prophet when his community in Mecca forced him to leave his birthplace. The *Muhajirun* – those who migrated with the Prophet from Mecca – saw themselves as the legitimate successors since they were kinsmen of the Prophet and the first to believe in his message. Through the mediation of Umar Ibn Al-Khattab, the conflict was settled by nominating Abu Bakr (632–34) from the *Muhajirun* as the first successor to the Prophet. However, this led to another conflict within the camp of the *Muhajirun* as the Prophet's family, the Banu Hashim, saw Ali Ibn Abi Taleb, the Prophet's cousin and son-in-law and the first convert to Islam, as the logical successor.

Abu Bakr was nominated by a small group of the elites of the Muslim community. The rest of the Muslims in Medina pledged their oath of public allegiance (*bay'a*) the following day in the Prophet's mosque. Abu Bakr was thus chosen by a method of limited choice that combined nomination by the elites of the community and affirmation by the members.

Abu Bakr himself circumvented this method of choosing a successor by nominating Umar (634–44) to succeed him. No consultation occurred and the *fait accompli* caused some ill-feeling in the community, particularly among Ali and his supporters.

Yet another method was utilized to select Uthman Ibn 'Affan', the third Khalife (644–56) (commonly spelt 'caliph' in English transliteration). Before his assassination, Umar refused to choose a successor, and stipulated that his own son could not succeed him. Instead, he established a Consultative Council, the Majlis Shura, to elect someone. Philip Hitti, the distinguished Arabist, has observed that the utilization of the Consultative Council, which included 'the oldest and most distinguished companions surviving, showed that the ancient Arabian idea of a tribal chief had triumphed over that of a hereditary monarch.'[2] All the members of the Council were appointed by Umar. An interesting feature of the Council was that all six members were contenders for the succession. They were Ali Ibn Abi Talib, Uthman Ibn 'Affan', Talha Ibn U'beidullah, al-Zubeir Ibn al-A'wwam, Sa'ad Ibn Abi Waqqas and Abdul Rahman Ibn A'wf. However, the committee's selection of Uthman did not allay discontent among the followers of Ali. A rebellion against Uthman ended in his assassination.

The rebellion against Uthman made Ali the fourth Khalife (656–61). This, in turn, led to the first open conflict between the Muslims in the battle of 'Al-Jamal' (the Camel) in 36 hijra (AD 656). Ali's succession also led to the second major confrontation, the Battle of Siffien (AD 657), between Ali's supporters and the supporters of Ma'awiyah Ibn Abi Sufian, who established the Umayyad dynasty (661–750).

The question of succession has thus been a source of conflict since the death of Muhammad. The Umayyads attempted to resolve this problem by establishing a hereditary system of succession. However, by the time of the establishment of the Umayyad dynasty, the Muslim community was permanently divided over the issue of succession into the Sunni and Shiah sects. The establishment of the Umayyad dynasty and the violent death of Ali's son Hussein, in 680, further widened the gap between the Sunnis and the Shiites and polarized their differences in religious and political matters. Commenting on the emergence of conflict within the Muslim community, Muhammad 'Umarah, has observed:

> Muslim differences emerged after the death of the Prophet on political issues, not religious issues. The differences centered around and resulted in conflict over the subject of Khalafah and the principle of government, particularly its political philosophy .... This political conflict was not only the first conflict but is the most fundamental of all conflicts. Muslims did not fight Muslims for religious reasons. They fought each other for political reasons.[3]

Khalafah or Imamah: The State in Islam

The problems of political succession following Muhammad's death reflect the fact that the Qur'ān did not provide guidelines on the form of the Islamic state. The need for the state is constructed on the principles of *Shari'a* (Islamic law) and *ijtihad* (reason). The basic argument of Islamic political thinkers in maintaining the necessity for the state in Islam derives from Islamic law (*Shari'a*), which in turn is based on the Qur'ān, the Sunna, tradition and analogy. The fact that Muhammad was a temporal ruler and his immediate followers chose a successor demonstrates that the institution of the state is essential. According to *Shari'a*, Muhammad maintained that 'A despotic ruler is better than anarchy'. Accordingly, the state is essential in order to prevent anarchy.

The rational part of the argument (*ijtihad*) for the necessity of the state derives from the basic premise that human beings are not capable of running their affairs harmoniously without the presence of a mediating authority. The proposition that 'Prophetic succession requires that the Imam exist among Muslims to protect their temporal interests, to protect their religion'[4] is one of the most basic in Islamic political thought. If anarchy is to be prevented and peace and justice are to prevail in the Islamic community, the state is necessary. According to a distinguished scholar of Islamic law and jurisprudence:

> Not only is Society regarded as indispensable for the survival of man, but also inherent in it is the concept of authority. Society, that is, cannot survive without authority. Indeed the Islamic conception of umma presupposes the existence of a set of divine commands, endowed by a Supreme Legislator, constituting its 'fundamental law' or 'constitution'. This is regarded as absolutely necessary since society without authority is impossible, for, though man is a social animal by nature, he is not a well-behaving animal. Has not Allah himself declared 'Men are the enemies of each other'? Has He not stated 'were it not for God [causing] the restraint of one man [by means] of another, the earth would have been corrupted?' The restraint upon man's social relations was enforced by authority and regulated by law; the latter was to show the beaten track to be trodden (and indeed the very term shari'a gives us this meaning) and the former as sanction for the enforcement of law.[5]

Both Sunnis and Shiites agree that the state is an essential institution. However, they fundamentally disagree over the nature of political legitimacy (*Khalafah* or *Imamah*) in the state. The word *Khalife* was originally used to denote a temporal role in the ruler's capacity to lead the political affairs of the community after the Prophet. The word Imam, in its simplest usage, refers to the leader of the Muslims at prayer. Thus, as it relates to the polity, it refers to the spiritual role of the ruler. A distinction between the two did not seem to represent a major political or religious problem in Islamic thought until the establishment of the Umayyad dynasty. The supporters of Ali, the Shiites, developed the doctrine of the Imamah later, to encompass both the religious and political dimensions of a true ruler. Although they continued to propagate the *Imamah* as reflected in the practice of the first four successors of the Prophet, the *Khalafah* did not seem to require any particular religious legitimacy in Sunni doctrine. It is true that he could still lead Muslims in their prayers, but this is a task that can be performed by any Muslim. In Sunni doctrine, political legitimacy derives from the acquisition of political power. 'Umarah effectively summarized the Sunni doctrine on the relationship between religious and temporal authority accordingly:

> The early Muslims, particularly the notable Companions of the Prophet, realized that the Prophet's death signified the conclusion of the era of prophecy . . . . Human beings after that have no right to speak in the name of the Creator or [claim] the divine [authority] that is installed upon the Prophet by his relationship to God . . . . With the death of the Prophet, the divine authority he possessed came to an end. No human being has the right to claim inheritance of this authority . . . . The Khalafah – which is the highest authority in the state – was based on consultation (shura), choice (ikhtiyar), contract (aqid) and allegiance (bay'a), and never on heredity . . . . There was an intention – in the beginning at least – to take it (Khalafah) away from the family of the Prophet so that political authority did not become associated with heredity in order to ensure that none of the Prophet's family at any time could assume the Prophet's religious power because they inherited his political authority. [The purpose was that] societal authorities and the State will not have a religious claim . . . . Thus, the Islamic position toward this important issue revolved around two principles: the first, religion, is what God revealed and transmitted to us in the Qur'an . . . second, what is temporal, political and legal which were not dealt with by the Qur'an . . . are left to ijtihad, the determining criteria and purpose of which should be the public interest – the interest of the entire community.[6]

The Shiites, however, maintain that political leadership of the Muslim community is primarily a religious function that belongs to the descendants of the Prophet and that Ali is the first Imam. Political legitimacy, in other words, fundamentally derives from religious legitimacy, which derives from God and is transmitted through the Prophet's line. A government based on any other foundation is a usurpation of God's temporal state. The Shiite doctrine of the *Imamah* derived from this principle. Furthermore, Shiite doctrine maintained that the Imam must be free from sin. His position of political authority rests upon spiritual leadership, for the state is primarily a spiritual entity. According to one of the most distinguished Shiite jurists, and the highest Shiite authority of the 1940s:

The Shiites added a fifth pillar to Islam – that is, the belief in Imamah. This means the Imam is a representative of God just like the prophets are his messengers. God chooses whomever he wants for the *Imamah* and orders his Prophet to appoint him. The Prophet appoints the Imam . . . to succeed the Prophet, to exercise all the duties that were conducted by the Prophet with the exception of revelation. He received all his instructions from the Prophet with divine direction. The Prophet gets his directives from God, and the Imam gets his directives from the Prophet. The Imamah is a chain of twelve, in which every Imam is appointed by his predecessor and appoints his successor. The Imam must be infallible, just like the Prophet . . . otherwise he forfeits [his legitimacy].[7]

Shiites believe *Imamah* is more encompassing than *Khalafah* and the Imam is the legitimate Khalife, whether he is in power or not. This is why the Shiite describe their ruler as only Khalife and their leaders as Imams. Imam is a title given by the Shiite *fuqaha* (jurists) who wrote on the topic. Thus, Sunni *fuqaha* who wrote on the topic used Shiite formulations for it. For example, al-Mawardi, in his most celebrated book *al-Ahkam al-Sultaniyah wa al-Wiliyat al-Diniyah* (Rules of Governments and Religious Succession), written in 450 hijra (AD 1058), begins his chapter on *Imamah* by defining it as an institution 'created to succeed prophecy for the purpose of guarding religion and managing society'.[8]

Commenting on the influence of Shiite political thought, Ahmad Mahmoud Subhi has observed:

The Sunnis were forced to deal with [the theory of] Imamah in response to the Shiites . . . , but the terms of this theory [of Imamah], its formulation and subjects were defined by the Shiites . . . . The works of other sects were limited to the propositions put forth by the Shiites . . . . The term Khalife is not used in Shiah work because it refers to those who usurped the right of the Prophet's family, as they believe . . . . Thus, Imamah became commonly used in philosophical works on political subjects, while the term Khalafah was limited to political history.[9]

Genealogy of Shiite Imams

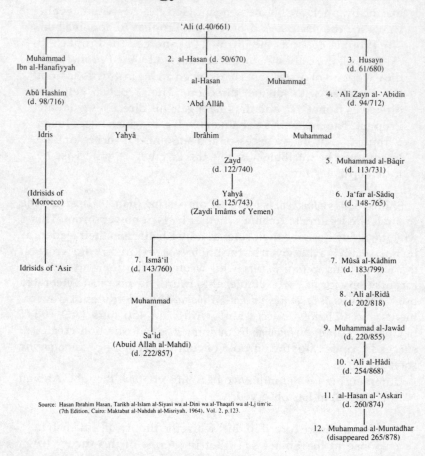

Source: Hasan Ibrahim Hasan, Tarikh al-Islam al-Siyasi wa al-Dini wa al-Thaqafi wa al-Lj tim'ie.
(7th Edition, Cairo: Maktabat al-Nahdah al-Misriyah, 1964), Vol. 2, p.123.

Political orthodoxy in classical Islam

The conflict over the question of succession led to the creation of two major sects in Islam – Sunna and Shiah. Fundamental to the schism between these sects was the issue of the nature of the Muslim state. As the doctrine of the state throughout the classical period, Sunni political thought represented political orthodoxy and developed as a paradigm of political studies. Shiah political thought, on the other hand, was articulated symbolically through the theological literature and thus did not develop a distinct school of political inquiry in this period.

As the official doctrine of the state, the Sunnis' political paradigm sought to recognize the legitimacy of the rule of the first four Khalifes. The Sunnis argued that the role of the Imam is essential, but they did not bestow on him the same mystical powers that the Shiites attributed to Imam Ali and the chain of Imams that followed him.[10] Unlike the Shiites, the Sunnis emphasized the doctrines of *shura* and *ahl al-hal wa al-'aqd* to justify their theory of the legitimacy of the rule of the four Khalifes.

The doctrine of *shura* is based on the Qur'ān, verse 159, Part IV, which directs the Prophet Muhammad to 'consult with them upon the conduct of affairs'; and verse 38, Part XXV refers to the followers of Islam as those 'whose affairs are a matter of counsel'. *Shura*, in this sense, was interpreted as a Consultative Council and as a check against despotic government.

During the Prophet's life, *shura* appears to have been practised, although no specific issues are delineated in the Qur'ān or the Sunna upon which the doctrine of *shura* must be invoked. What seems to have occurred is that Muhammad consulted a council of his followers in an *ad hoc* manner on issues as they arose. The *shura* came into formal existence during Umar's Khalifate, for the specific purpose of choosing a successor. Umar gave the following instructions to a council of six on how to elect a successor. 'If five agree and one dissents, chop his head; if four agree and two disagree, chop their heads; if three agree and three dissent, then my son Abdullah shall have the final say in choosing one of the three as a successor. Whoever disagrees after that must be killed.'[11]

The difficulties arising from the vagueness of the concept of *shura* and the lack of political institution or formal structure through which the *shura* could be practised led Muslim theoreticians to search for a solution. The solution was the concept of *ahl al-hal wa al-'aqd* (Council of Notables),[12] to be the basis for a legitimate method of choosing a leader.

The early formulations of the concept emphasized the role of the religious leaders as the only ones qualified to belong to the category of ahl al-hall wa al-'aqd. The following were considered to be the criteria for membership: justice; knowledge that is sufficient to enable the member to ascertain the qualifying abilities of a candidate for the office of the Khalife; reason and prudence that leads to a choice of the best candidate.[13]

Later, however, Muslim theoreticians changed their criteria and *ahl al-hal wa al-'aqd* meant, in practice, the elite and prominent members of the Muslim community, irrespective of their religious merits. This concept of *ahl al-hal wa al-'aqd* was never clearly defined. How were the members to be chosen? What was their role? What was the relationship of this group to the rest of the Muslim community? These and other questions were never clearly answered, a fact which has led to political turmoil throughout Islamic history. The continuity of this concept and the ineffectiveness of the Consultative Council (*shura*) became obvious when the *Khalafah* was made into a royal dynasty under the Umayyads. This was even true long before that, when the Consultative Council and the wise men of the Islamic community were beset by intrigues, personal ambitions, and even class interest.[14] Thus, under the doctrine of *ahl al-hal wa al-'aqd*, the Muslim community was constantly faced by a *fait accompli* in the issue of succession, and prevented from playing an active political role in choosing the ruler. As a result, dissension, rebellion and factionalism erupted with each succession.

The dominant issues of classical Sunni political theory centred around establishing the fundamental legitimacy of the first four Khalifes, including the mechanisms of their selection, and the problems of public administration that derived from these models: what were the qualities essential in a ruler; how many people should belong to *ahl al-hal wa al-'aqd*; how many constituted a legal *bay'a*, and what constituted *ijma* (consensus). With the expansion of the dynastic state, the increasing distance between the ruler and the community made the problem of the public interest a central concern in these issues: what was the public interest; how was it best served; what if it was violated? Within this framework, the contrasting views of two influential Sunni theorists, Abu Bakr Muhammad Ibn al-Tayyeb al-Baqelani (died AD 1013) and Shehab al-Din Ahmad Ibn Abi al-Rabi'a (who lived sometime between the ninth and thirteenth centuries),[15] are representative of the scope and nature of these debates.

Al-Baqelani maintained that the Imam should be chosen by the *ahl al-hal wa al-'aqd*. The nomination could be made by one person, and the *bay'a* achieved by consensus. While he stressed that the Imam should be among the most pious, knowledgeable and respected members of the community, and a member of the Quraysh tribe, he did not have to be considered infallible. Thus, the community can legitimately depose an Imam for a number of reasons: if he reverts to atheism or stops praying and encourages others to do the same; for tyranny and corruption, insanity, deafness or muteness, senility; if he becomes a prisoner of war for a long period, or it is believed that this will endanger the interests of the nation.[16]

What al-Baqelani represents is that group of Sunni theorists who, disquieted by the abuses of dynastic rule, while still not directly challenging its legitimacy, saw the community as the state, not the ruler. Thus, they conceptualized the ruler more as a public servant who could be deposed in the interests of the community. What they stressed, however, was not the disposition of the ruler, but his selection – both the process and the criteria. Nevertheless, the proposition that the Imam could be deposed for incapacity – physical or moral – in the performance of his duties was an explicit statement regarding the nature of government. This was obviously, if implicitly, a position of opposition to the status quo of the dynastic rule that had evolved in the Islamic state, but not clearly a position of opposition to its legitimacy.

Al-Rabi'a represents the opposite position among Sunni theorists. This position derived from the assumption of the fundamental legitimacy of the ruler and the community's consequent responsibility to honour and obey him. In his seminal book *Suluk al-Malik fi Tadbir al-Mamalik*, al-Rabi'a maintained: 'God has bestowed upon the kings his blessings and made it possible for them to control His lands. He entrusted them with his followers. This requires the ulamas to glorify the kings and to honour them . . . . God also made it required of them to obey the kings.'[17]

This position essentially conceptualizes the ruler as state and the community as servant of the state. While al Rabi'a considered the ideal personal qualities of a ruler, he was more concerned about the administration of the state, maintaining that the administration must be the source of corruption since the ruler is above corruption.[18] His book is a compendium of advice to the king on effective administration. What it represents is a disavowal of the proposition that the community has any right to disobey a ruler and an alternative administrative explanation of the problems that plagued the community under dynastic rule.

The contrary conceptions of community as state and ruler as state represented in the works of al-Baqelani and al-Rabi'a reflected efforts within the Sunni school to reconcile the contradictions of state and community that were already manifest in the Islamic empire. As the orthodox school of Islam, the Sunni school took as unproblematic the nature of the state and concentrated on discovering the true form of government in addressing these contradictions. At the same time, however, there were Sunni scholars commenting on the works of the ancient Greek philosophers such as Plato and Aristotle. They added a more analytic and speculative dimension by contemplating the possibility of different forms of government in the state. Abu Nasr

Muhammad al-Farabi (870–950) is considered to be the founder of this philosophic 'school'.

Al-Farabi formulated a science of government, conceptualized in the following quotation from his influential work *Ihsa al-Ulum*:[19]

> Political Science investigates the various kinds of voluntary actions and ways of life; the positive dispositions, morals, inclinations, and states of character that lead to these actions and ways of life; the ends for the sake of which they are performed; how they must exist in man; how to order them in man in the manner in which they must exist in him; and the way to preserve them for him. It distinguishes among the ends for the sake of which actions are performed and the ways of life are practised. It explains that some of them are true happiness, while others are presumed to be happiness although they are not. That which is true happiness cannot possibly be of this life, but of another life after this, which is the life to come; while that which is presumed to be happiness consists of such things as wealth, honor, and the pleasures, when these are made the only ends in this life. Distinguishing the actions and ways of life, it explains that the ones through which true happiness is attained are the good, noble things, and the virtues, while the rest are the evil, base things, and the imperfections; and that they [must] exist in man in such a way that the virtuous actions and ways of life are distributed in the cities and nations according to a certain order and are practised in common. It explains that this comes about only through a rulership (ri'asah) by which [the ruler] establishes these actions, ways of life, states of character, positive dispositions, and morals in the cities and nations, and endeavours to preserve them so that they do not perish; and that this rulership comes about only by virtue of a craft and a positive disposition that leads to the actions that establish [these virtues], and to the actions that preserve what has been established among them [that is, the cities and nations]. This is the royal craft or kingship, or whatever one chooses to call it; politics (siyasah) is the operation of this craft.

From this, al-Farabi developed a classification of political regimes:

- the Virtuous Cities, where the purposes of government and the institutions of society (ways of life) are organized on the basis of the attainment of true happiness (that is, happiness as revealed by God).

- the Ignorant Cities, where government is ignorant of the nature of true happiness and the institutions of society are organized on other bases: the attainment of necessities (indispensable city), wealth (vile city), pleasure (base city), honour (timocratic city), domination (despotic city), or freedom (democratic city).
- the Immoral Cities, where the government is cognizant of the nature of true happiness but does not adhere to this, and the institutions of society are organized for the attainment of other ends, as in the Ignorant Cities.
- The Erring Cities, where the purposes of government are displaced from the attainment of true happiness and the institutions of society are being corrupted.[20]

Like other Sunni political thinkers, al-Farabi was concerned with the problems of defining the best government for the Muslim community. His 'virtuous city', the ideal society, can be defined as:

a regime in which men come together and cooperate with the aim of becoming virtuous, performing noble activities, and attaining happiness. It is distinguished by the presence of knowledge of man's ultimate perfection, the distinction between the noble and the base and between the virtues and the vices, and the concerted effort of the rulers and the citizens to teach and learn these things, and to develop the virtuous forms or states of character from which emerge the noble activities useful for achieving happiness.[21]

All other regimes were defined in contrast to the virtuous city. This implicitly provided a framework for evaluating any society prior to Islam, and any political regime within the Islamic world. While al-Farabi himself cautiously refrained from making explicit references to any rulers in the Islamic world, his specification of the attributes of the ideal ruler was clearly an implicit affirmation of the rule of the first four Khalifes. In addition, his discussion of the responsibilities of the ruler *vis-à-vis* the community provided an implicit condemnation of the abuses of government in subsequent regimes.

Al-Farabi defined the ideal government in the ideal society – the 'virtuous city' – as a non-hereditary monarchy or aristocracy and advocated the idea of Plato's Philosopher King. He listed twelve attributes of the ruler, '*ra'is awwal*', but would be satisfied with one who had five or six. In case there were no people with even that minimum number of attributes, then a council of two to six possessing an aggregate of ten attributes should be chosen. One of them should be a 'hakim' (wise-man), to know the needs of the state and the people.[22]

Without the proper ruler, a virtuous city could be transformed into another type – erring or immoral. In effect, what al-Farabi posited was a theory of transformation of societies that identified the temporal forces amenable to human intervention. By carefully distinguishing between the realms of human and divine action, al-Farabi identified where man is responsible for the state of society and human intervention possible. Furthermore, he laid this responsibility on the head of government. However, he left to God the correction of an immoral or erring ruler, in effect side-tracking the issue of direct human intervention in the transformation of government.[23]

The philosophic school reconciled philosophy and theology. This provided the basis for a science of government that allowed the discourse to move beyond the seeming contradictions of community and state, human intervention and divine intervention, philosophy and theology. Most significantly, reform of society could be legitimated on theological and rational grounds and revolution rationalized on theological grounds.

The critical problems of public administration that developed with the rapid expansion of the state from community to empire, the progressive degradation of the real power of the Khalife and the increasing disintegration of the empire, are reflected in the increasing attention given to the issue of public administration by Sunni political thinkers. Abu al-Hassan al-Mawardi (974–1058) was one of the most prominent and influential advocates of public administration reform. He wrote a number of works on politics, the most famous of which are *al-Ahkam Sultaniyah*, *Nasihat al-Muluk*, and *Qawanin al-Wizarah*. Al-Mawardi considered the *Imamah* to be a 'caliphate of prophethood in safeguarding religious and temporal affairs.'[24] *Imamah* is the foundation of the community and is necessary by the *Shari'a* and by reason to maintain the commuity on the 'right path' – that is, to establish the rules and regulations on which the community depends. The Imam, or the personification of *Imamah*, should be characterized by the following: justice, knowledge for the purposes of 'ijtihad', no handicaps in his physical or sense faculties, wisdom in ruling the community and running its affairs, courage to protect Islam and fight its enemies and, finally, descent from Quraysh.[25]

The Iman can be chosen either by election by *ahl al-hal wa al-'aqd* or by appointment by the previous Imam. The Imam has to vow to perform his duties (*'ahd*), and the community must pledge its allegiance (*bay'a*) and obedience. The role of the Imam is to protect the faith, to adjudicate among people, to punish transgressors, to appoint honest administrators, and should take a middle path between luxury and total dedication to prayer. The Imam can only be removed for one of two reasons: *'hajr'* and *'qahr'*. *Hajr* means the Imam falling under the influence of one of his assistants who might act contrary to the teachings of Islam and justice, while *'qahr'* means the Imam falls prisoner to the hands of a 'formidable enemy' and there is no hope of saving or freeing him.[26]

Al-Mawardi's unique contribution was his elaboration of a structure of government administration. He lists two kinds of *'wizara'* or ministries: *'wizarat Tafwidh'* (delegation) and *'wizarat Tanfith'* (execution). Since the minister of *Tafwidh* is the chief administrator of the state, he must have all the qualities of the Imam, except the condition of descent from Quraysh. In addition he should have knowledge of military affairs and tax collection (*kharaj*). In many ways, al-Marawdi seemed to consider this position to be more powerful than that of the Imam. Orders issued by this minister could not be overruled by the Imam unless they were contrary to established legal practice. However, the minister of *Tafwidh* cannot appoint his successor and can be dismissed by the Imam.

The minister of *Tanfith* is a 'middle man between the Imam and his subjects and the governors.'[27] His main function is to execute the decrees of the Iman. Thus, his position is directly subordinated to the Khalife and much less powerful than the minister of *Tafwidh*. Mawardi lists eight main qualities of persons occupying the position of the minister of *Tanfith*, but the latter does not have to be a Muslim.

Governors of provinces (*Amir*) can be appointed by the Imam. This *'imara'* (governorship) is of two kinds: general and special. The general *imara* is divided again into two types: first, *Imarat Istikfa'* which is an appointment by the Imam of his own free will; second, *Imarat Istila'*, an appointment which is forced on the Imam if any *Amir* controls a province by force. The 'special *imara'* is limited to the affairs of the army, defence of the community and safeguarding women, but this *imara* cannot deal with matters of justice, religious laws, or taxes.[28]

Al-Mawardi lists four main departments: the Army Board, the Board of Provincial Boundaries, the Board of Appointment and Dismissal of Officers, and the Treasury. Justice must be administered by an independent judge who must have certain qualities, two of which are honesty and being a Muslim.[29]

The significance of al-Mawardi lies in his conception of the *Khalafah*. He provided a functional distinction between the position of Khalife as titular head of state and the institutions of government as the effective power of the state. In effect, al-Mawardi's perspective placed more significance on the structure of government than on the Imam in the performance of the functions of the state. His conception of public administration as a rationally ordered tool of the *Khalafah* established a direct relationship between the Sunni theory of *Khalafah* and the institutions of government.[30]

As these works reflect, all of the Sunni political thinkers idealized the rule of the first four Khalifes as a paragon of Islamic government and society, and attempted to solve contemporary problems by deriving principles from these models. As Islamic society itself became more complex – evolving from a culturally homogeneous tribal community to a culturally heterogeneous empire, from a united state to a dissassembled region of competing principalities – the theological, juridical and philosophic derivations became increasingly convoluted. Furthermore, religion, state, society and culture were all modified by their adaptations to regional and local, social, political and cultural variations in the empire. Thus, the contrast between the idealized society of the first four Khalifes and the contemporary society of the dynastic empires was all the more profound. A reaction to the modifications of Islam developed, especially among some theological scholars who rejected derivations from the ideal to the real as constituting rationalizations for the compromise of Islam and adaptations as deviations from Islam. They blamed the corruption and decay they perceived around them on the dilution of original principles. Ahmad Ibn Taymiyah (1260–1327) was one of the most outspoken advocates of a return to the original creed and practices of early Islam.

Arguing that the Qur'ān, the Sunna and the behaviour of the *Salaf* (first three generations of Islam) define the basis of Islamic life, Ibn Taymiyah maintained that everything else represented innovation (*bid'a*) and should therefore be censured.[31] How this related to his attitudes towards government is revealed in his observation that 'those who desire to dominate people and corrupt the earth . . . are malfeasors. They are the kings and corrupt rulers just like the pharaoh and his entourage. They are the most immoral people.'[32] Ibn Taymiyah regarded all rulers who followed the first four Khalifes in this light. He did not consider obedience to a corrupt ruler to be necessary;[33] indeed, he did not consider the Khalife necessary.

Rather, he argued that the qualities Sunni writers considered essential in a Khalife could only be found in the *Salaf*. Thus, the *Khalafah* was a fiction that mystified organized tyranny. What is needed of government is the performance of the functions of applying the *Shari'a* and promotion and protection of the spiritual and material well-being of the community. Ibn Taymiyah utilized the term '*wilayah*' to refer to the empowerment of government in the performance of these functions. Those who hold public office are empowered to perform their duties as representatives of God. They are entrusted to ensure the rule of justice and well-being of the community. At their head is an Imam (learned jurist) who is responsible for the organization of government. Government departments can be created by the Imam, according to his judgement of need and utility.[34]

Ibn Taymiyah did not consider it necessary for the community to elect an Imam. The important characteristic of the Imam's empowerment is the *bay'a*, a bilateral contract between the Imam and the *ahl al-hal wa al-'aqd* that is binding on the community. The condition that the Imam has to be of Quraysh descent runs contrary to the Islamic teaching of equality among Muslims. The mandate of the Imam is the implementation of divine law. Justice, the community's well-being, social stability and safeguarding the rights of the individual are, Ibn Taymiyah maintained, the prerequisites for God's favourable consideration and protection of any state even though that state might not be a Muslim one.[35]

Arguing from a juristic perspective that the Qur'ān clearly specified that the basis of government is consultation (*Shura*), and from a rational perspective that the foundation of government is co-operation, Ibn Taymiyah maintained that the Imam must implement and abide by consultations to a greater extent than had generally been practised throughout Islamic history. The Consultative Council should be representative of both the *ulama* (Muslim jurists) and leaders of public opinion.

In essence, Ibn Taymiyah argued that the government is responsible to the community to implement divine law, and the community is responsible to God to maintain a government that implements divine law. This reasoning provided a theological and rational basis for both government legitimacy and revolutionary legitimacy: it is a Muslim's duty to obey a government that implements divine law and to oppose a government that engages in innovation or deviation from divine law. Ibn Taymiyah's contribution to Islamic political theory was seminal for it became the ideological foundation of the Salafiyah movement and contemporary Islamic activist movements (both to be discussed later).

Ibn Khaldun (1332–1406) is the final classical Sunni political thinker to be considered here. Living in a period of great political upheaval and social strife, he perceived a cyclical motion and sociological process in the rise and fall of not only Islamic states but of civilizations generally. The uniqueness of his method and the significance of his work earned him the position of a founder of modern social science and cultural history.

Unlike other classical Sunni political thinkers, Ibn Khaldun focused directly on the issue of the nature of the state, identifying the power of force as its foundation and group solidarity (*asabiyya*), based on natural kinship, worldly desires and religion, as its origin. Strong group cohesiveness leads to the establishment of the superiority of one group over others. 'This is because aggressive and defensive strength is obtained only through group feeling, which means affection and willingness to fight and die for each other.'[36] This superiority was manifested in the establishment of organized authority (government) which took the form of dynastic or royal authority at that time. The dissipation of a ruling group's solidarity over time as a result of a human proclivity to increasing preoccupation with worldly desires leads to the weakening of government authority and vulnerability to displacement by groups with stronger group cohesiveness. In this way, the motion of the rise and fall of states is cyclical.

The nature of government derives from the form of a state and is manifest in the system of authority imposed to maintain the state. Malcolm Kerr has summarized Ibn Khaldun's theory of government accordingly:[37]

He first of all uses the term mulk to denote political control in human society as a generic term. This is divided into mulk tabi'i and mulk siyasi. Mulk tabi'i or 'natural sovereignty' denotes the unregulated exercise of power by a ruler based on sheer force, only one step removed from the law of the jungle. Mulk siyasi or 'political sovereignty' is rule by law, or nomocracy. It is subdivided into two types: siyasa 'aqliyya or rationally derived nomocracy, and siyasa diniyya or religiously derived nomocracy. The Caliphate is of the latter type.

Ibn Khaldun's theory of *Khalafah* derived from his propositions regarding the nature of the state and the nature of government and it represented a specific case of his general theory of government. Concerned primarily with the process of change within the institution of government, he examined the transition of the *Khalafah* from communal to royal authority and the processes of disintegration that dissipated royal authority. 'Any royal authority must be built upon two foundations. The first is might and group feeling, which finds its expression in soldiers. The second is money, which supports the soldiers and provides the whole structure needed by royal authority. Disintegration befalls the dynasty at these two foundations.'[38]

What distinguished Islamic government from other forms of government were the following: (1) the nature of the Islamic state, which subordinates both group solidarity and power to divine law, and (2) the nature of Islamic government, which subordinates temporal political authority to the maintenance of the welfare of the Islamic community. While Islamic law is universal, eternal and perfect, human beings are particularistic, mortal and imperfect – characteristics that produce inherent human tendencies toward the perverse and the profane. It is this aspect of human nature that makes Islamic government necessary. But since government itself is a temporal institution, run by human beings, it is subject to these same tendencies. As a result, the process of development, growth and decay of the *Khalafah* is cyclical:

We have stated that the life of a dynasty does not as a rule extend beyond three generations. The first generation retains the desert qualities, desert toughness, and desert savagery. [Its members are used to] privation and to sharing their glory [with each other]; they are brave and rapacious. Therefore, the strength of group feeling continues to be preserved among them. They are sharp and greatly feared. People submit to them.

Under the influence of royal authority and a life of ease, the second generation changes from the desert attitude to sedentary culture, from privation to luxury and plenty, from a state in which everybody shares in the glory to one in which one man claims all the glory for himself while the others are too lazy to strive for glory, and from proud superiority to humble subservience. Thus, the vigour of group feeling is broken to some extent. People become used to lowliness and obedience. But many of the old virtues remain in them, because they had had direct personal contact with the first generation and its conditions, and had observed with their own eyes its prowess and striving for glory and its intention to protect and defend [itself]. They cannot give all of it up at once, although a good deal of it may go. They live in hope that the conditions that existed in the first generation may come back, or they live under the illusion that those conditions still exist.

The third generation, then, has [completely] forgotten the period of desert life and toughness, as if it had never existed. They have lost [the taste for] the sweetness of fame and for group feeling, because they are dominated by force. Luxury reaches its peak among them, because they are so much given to a life of prosperity and ease. They become dependent on the dynasty and are like women and children who need to be defended. Group feeling disappears completely. People forget to protect and defend themselves and to press their claims. With their emblems, apparel, horseback-riding, and [fighting] skill, they deceive people and give them the wrong impression. For the most part, they are more cowardly than women upon their backs. When someone comes and demands something from them, they cannot repel him. The ruler, then, has need of other, brave people to support him. He takes many clients and followers. They help the dynasty to some degree, until God permits it to be destroyed, and it goes with everything it stands for.[39]

Notes

1. Muhammad 'Umarah, *al-Islam wa al-Sultah al-Dinyah*, 2nd edn, Beirut, al-Mosasah al-Arabiyah lil-Dirasat wa al-Nashir, 1980, pp. 46–7.
2. Philip Hitti, *History of the Arabs*, 8th edn, London, Macmillan, 1963.
3. Muhammad 'Umarah, *al-Khalafah wa Nashaat al-Ahzab al-Islamiyah*, Beirut, al-Mosasah al-Arabiyal lil-Dirasat wa al-Nishir, August 1977, p. 70.
4. Muhammad Ahmed Abu Zahra, *al-Mathahib al-Islamiyah*, Cairo, Ministry of Education, 'One Thousand Books' series, 1957, p. 31.
5. Majid Khadduri, *War and Peace in the Law of Islam*, Baltimore, Johns Hopkins Press, 1955, p. 5.
6. 'Umarah, op. cit., pp. 14–18.
7. Imam Muhammad al-Hussain Ahl Kashif al-Ghata, *Asil al-Shi'a wa Isoliha*, Najaf, al-Haydariyah Press, p. 97.
8. Abu al-Hasan, *'Ali ibn Muhammad ibn Habib al-Mawardi*, Beirut, Dar al-Kutub al-Ilmiyah, 1978.
9. Ahmad Mahmoud Subhi, *Nadhariyat al-Imamah Inda al-Shi'a al-Ithnay 'Ashriya*, Cairo, Dar al-Ma'aref, 1969, pp. 22–4.
10. See the views of Abu al-Hassan al-Ash'ari in Yusuf Ibish, *Nusual-fikr al-*

siyasi al-Islami, 'Tests of Islamic Political Theory', Beirut, Dar al-Tali'a, 1966, pp. 19–26.

11. Ibn Qutaiba, *al-Imamah wa al-Siyasah*, 1, Cairo, Al-Halabi & Co., Institute for Publishing and Distribution, 1967, p. 29.

12. Ahl al-hal wa al-'aqd, literally translated, means 'those who loosen and bind', i.e. those entrusted with the authority to make binding decisions.

13. al-Mawardi, op. cit., p. 43.

14. See Ahmad Abbas Saleh, *al-Yamin wa al-Yasar fi al-Islam* (The Right and the Left in Islam), 2nd edn, Beirut, al-Mo'asasa al-Arabiyah lil-Dirasat wa al-Nashir, 1973, pp. 51–87.

15. For a discussion of the controversy over the period of al-Rabi'a's life, see Muhammad Jalal Sharaf, *Nashat al-Fikr al-Syasi wa Tatworhu fi al-Islam*, Beirut, Dar al-Nahdha al-Arabiyah, 1982, pp. 141–4.

16. Abu Bakr Muhammad Ibn al-Tayyeb al-Baqelani, 'Selected Writing', in Yusif Ibish (ed.), *Nisus al-Fikr al-Syasi al-Islami: al-Imamah 'ind al-Sunna*, Beirut, Dar al-Tali'ah, August 1966, pp. 55–8.

17. Shehab al-Din Ahmad Ibn abi al-Rabi'a, *Suluk al-Malik fi Tadbir al-Mamalik*, Cairo, n.p., 1286 hijra, pp. 99–100.

18. Ibid., pp. 116–17.

19. Abu Nasr Muhammad al-Farabi, 'On Political Science, Jurisprudence and Dialectical Theory', in Ralph Lerner and Muhsin Mahdi, *Medieval Political Philosophy: A Sourcebook*, New York, The Free Press, 1963, p. 24.

20. Abu Nasr Muhammad al-Farabi, *Ara ahl al-Madinah al-Fadhilah*, Cairo, Faraj Allah al-Kurdi, 1323 hijra, pp. 90–3. For an excellent English translation, see Al-Farabi, 'The Political Regime', in Lerner and Mahdi, *Medieval Political Philosophy*, pp. 32–53.

21. Muhsin Mahdi, 'Al-Farabi', in Leo Strauss and Joseph Gropsey et al., *History of Political Philosophy*, Chicago, Rand McNally, 1963, p. 164.

22. al-Farabi, op. cit., pp. 87–90.

23. Omar Farokh, *Turikh al-Fikr al-Arabi*, Beirut, Dar al-Ilm lil Malayen, 1966, pp. 372–4.

24. Abi al-Hassan Ali Bin Muhammad Bin Habib al-Bassri al Baghdadi al-Mawardi, *Al-Ahkam al-Sultaniyah wa al-Wiliyah al-Diniyah*, Beirut, Dar al-Kutub al-Ilmiyah, 1978, p. 5.

25. Ibid., p. 6.

26. Ibid., p. 25.

27. Ibid., p. 25.

28. Ibid., pp. 30–4.

29. Ibid., pp. 60–5.

30. Said Binsaid, *Dawlat al-Khalafah: Dirasah fi al-Tafkir al-Siyasi ind al-Mawardi*, Casablanca, Dar al-Nashr al-Maghribiyah, n.d., pp. 157–8.

31. Muhammad Umar Memon, *Ibn Taimiya's Struggle Against Popular Religion*, Paris, Mouton, 1976, pp. 5–7.

32. Ahmad Bin Taymiyah, *Majmo' Fatawi Sheikh al-Islam Ahmad Bin Taymiyah*, **28**, Rabaat, al-Ma'arif Press, 1981, p. 392.

33. Ibid., **10**, p. 266.

34. Haroon Khan Sherwani, *Studies in Muslim Political Thought and Administration*, Philadelphia, Porcupine Press, 1977, pp. 169–84.

35. Ibid.

36. Malcolm H. Kerr, *Islamic Reform: The Political and Legal Theories of Muhammad 'Abduh and Rashid Rida*, Berkeley, University of California Press, 1966, p. 123.
37. Ibid., p. 29.
38. Ibn Khaldun, *The Mugaddimah: An Introduction to History*, trs. Franz Rosenthal, Princeton, Princeton University Press, 1967, p. 246.
39. Ibid., p. 137.

2 Reformist Islam*

The classical paradigm of politics was founded on an image of the state that presupposed religion as the source of power and *Khalafah* as the framework of government. Under the Ottoman empire (1252–1914), the unity of the Islamic state was re-established and its domain expanded to its apex (1517). However, the Ottomans dispensed altogether with *Khalafah* as the framework of government. In effect, the classical paradigm was rendered irrelevant by the seeming contradiction between substance (state) and form (government). For a time, political thought lost its dynamism.

However, by the seventeenth century, the power of the Ottoman empire was being fundamentally checked and challenged by the emerging West. Furthermore, effective government administration within the empire was being dissipated by the excesses of luxury and abuses of power. In this atmosphere of intensifying external challenge and internal decay, Islamic political thought was revitalized. The Salafiyah movements of the eighteenth and nineteenth century, reformers of the nineteenth century and nationalists of the twentieth century trace their intellectual roots to the classical paradigm of politics.

The Salafiyah movement, a religious movement dedicated to the puritanical reform of Muslim society, was philosophically founded on the work of Ibn Taymiyah. In the seventeenth, eighteenth and nineteenth centuries, a number of Salafiyah cults crystallized into significant political forces: the Wahhabi movement of the Arabian Peninsula, the Shawkani movement of Yemen, the Sanusi movement of Libya, and the Mahdi movement of the Sudan. In each of these cases, Salafiyah doctrine became the ideological basis of unification of the population and mobilization to effectively challenge existing power. The expansion

---

* This chapter draws largely on the monumental works of Fahmi Jad'an, *Usus a-Taqadum 'inda Mufkiri al-Islam fi al-Alam al-'Arabi al-Hadith*, Beirut, al-Mu'asasah al-Arabiyah lil-Dirasat wa al-Nashir, 1979; and Albert Hourani, *Arabic Thought in the Liberal Age, 1798–1939*, London, Oxford University Press, 1962.

of each movement was ultimately checked by confrontation with the imperialist powers. Islamic political thought subsequently became preoccupied with the problems of modernization.

Modernization reformers

The Salafiyah movements of the eighteenth and nineteenth centuries had arisen as a conservative religious reaction within Islam to a perceived corruption of the Islamic faith. This corruption was, more often than not, seen to be primarily internal in nature – the result of Ottoman decadence and the declining zeal (and orthodoxy) of the *ulama*. In contrast, the Islamic intellectual reformers of the nineteenth and early twentieth centuries were motivated by an external challenge to Islam: the decline of the Ottoman empire and the concomitant expansion of European influence in the Middle East. Such reformers sought to analyse and rectify the apparent political, military, technological, and economic shortcomings of the Islamic world, thereby strengthening it *vis-à-vis* the West. Because the stimuli differed, the geographic centre of gravity of the movements and the later reformers also differed. The former had been born in Arabia, Yemen, the Sudan and Libya – areas where Islamic traditionalism was strong and European influence relatively weak. The latter, on the other hand, most often arose in areas such as Egypt where European influence had become particularly established.

Two of the earliest prominent thinkers to deal with the question of Islamic weakness in the modern world were Rifa'a al-Tahtawi (1801–73) and Khayr al-Din al-Tunisi (1810–90). The lives and philosophical development of both these men illustrate well the fundamental role that European influence played in the development of intellectual reformism in Islam.

Rifa'a al-Tahtawi was an al-Azhar-educated Egyptian who was appointed by Muhammad Ali as an Imam with the first major Egyptian mission to France in 1826. There he studied European science and philosophy, becoming acquainted with the works of Voltaire, Rousseau, Montesquieu, and other leaders of eighteenth-century French thought. When he returned to Egypt in 1831 he wrote a critical appraisal of the strengths and weaknesses of French society, *Takhlis al-Ibriz ila Takhlis Bariz*. Thereafter, he translated a number of European works into Arabic and wrote a number of additional works of his own, including *Manahii al-albab al-misriyya fi mabahij al-adab*, a treatise on Egyptian development.

Al-Tahtawi was one of the first people to seriously encourage the adoption of modern European scientific thought for the development of the Islamic world. In the introduction to his book on his travels in France, *Takhlis al-Ibriz ila Takhlis Bariz,* he noted 'I have written this book to encourage the Muslim land to understand foreign science, industry and arts.... During my stay in the country of the French, I felt sad that they enjoy [a higher standard of living] that is non-existent in the Islamic lands.'[1]

Khayr al-Din was a Circassian Mameluke who rose to the highest government ranks in Tunis, and later in Constantinople. He spent four years in Paris in the service of Ahmed Bey of Tunis, and when he returned to Tunis in 1856 he became one of Bey's ministers. In 1859, and again in 1864 and 1871, he travelled to Constantinople in an attempt to offset French pressure on Tunis by strengthening its ties to the Sublime Porte within the Ottoman empire. When he lost Ahmed Bey's favour in 1877 and was dismissed from his positions, he moved to Constantinople and served as grand vizier to Sultan Abdulhamid until 1879. Khayr al-Din's major theoretical contribution to the reformism of the era was his *Aqwam al-masalik fi ma'rifat ahwal al-mamalik.* In it, Khayr al-Din set himself two tasks:

> The first task is to spur on those statesmen and savants having zeal and resolution to seek all possible ways of improving the conditions of the Islamic umma [community] and of promoting the means of its development by such things as expanding the scope of sciences and knowledge, smoothing the paths to wealth in agriculture and commerce, promoting all the industries and eliminating the causes of idleness. The basic requirement is good government from which is born that security, hope and proficiency in work to be seen in the European kingdoms. No further evidence is needed of this.
>
> The second task is to warn the heedless among the Muslim masses against their persistent opposition to the behaviour of others that is praiseworthy and in conformity with our Holy Law simply because they are possessed with the idea that all behaviour and organizations of non-Muslims must be renounced, their books must be cast out and not mentioned, and anyone praising such things should be disavowed. This attitude is a mistake under any circumstances.[2]

Although al-Tahtawi, Khayr al-Din and their contemporaries were the first to attempt to secularize Western science and technology, in effect separating issues of social development from religious issues. However, the issues were soon confounded by the problem of imperialism. Jamal al-Din al-Afghani (c. 1839–96), Muhammad 'Abduh (1849–1905) and Rashid Redha (1865–1935) played a fundamental role in formulating an Islamic response to the twin problems of domestic development and Western imperialism. Their doctrines – formulated at a time when European pressure on the Islamic world had reached new heights with the Russo–Turkish war (1877), the French occupation of Tunis (1881), and the British occupation of Egypt (1882) – were to have a lasting effect on social and political thought in the Islamic world, and one which can be seen to the present day.

Jamal al-Din al-Afghani was born in Sadabad, Afghanistan. Over the course of his turbulent political career he served governments in Afghanistan, Istanbul, Egypt and Persia. He invariably came into conflict with the ruler in power and was banished. During one of his exiles in Paris, he established a society, Jamiyat al-Urwa al-Wathqa, advocating an Islamic awakening and revolution.

Al-Afghani's primary concerns were with the disunity, corruption and weakness of the Islamic world in the face of Western imperialism. To a large extent he blamed the state of Islamic society on the corruption of Islamic leadership which had allowed superstition and ignorance to replace reason and enlightenment in the guidance of society: 'Religion and science cannot disagree. If it appears as such, we must employ exegesis. Ignorance and rigidity are so abundant among those who don the cloak of ulama that they allege that the Qur'ān contradicts scientific facts .... The Qur'ān disavows such allegations. The Qur'ān must transcend contradictions with real science.'[3]

Rather than trying to secularize the issues of Western science and technology, al-Afghani attempted to synthesize them with Islamic thought. His ideas of Islamic awakening amid corrupt political-religious establishments advocated radical reformism, if not revolution. Afghani's ideas reflected the strong influence of Salafiyah thought in his diagnosis of the corruption and decay of Islamic society, and in his prescription of purification to revitalize the dynamic spirit of Islam to meet the challenge posed by the West.

Muhammad Abduh was born in Egypt in 1849 and educated at al-Azhar University, the centre of higher Islamic studies in the Muslim world. A close friend and ideological ally of al-Afghani, Abduh struggled for revolution in Egypt. He actively supported Ahmad

Urabi's revolution in 1882 and, on its failure, was jailed briefly, then exiled for six years. While in exile in Paris, 'Abduh joined al-Afghani in the secret society, Jamiyat al-Urwa al-Wathqa, and the publication of its newspapers. By the time he returned to Egypt in 1889, however, Abduh had despaired of revolution or reform. He devoted himself entirely to philanthropic activities.

Abduh's revolutionary activism was focused on Egypt, though his ideological perspective derived from the broad framework of the Islamic *umma*. His primary concerns were with nation-building and British imperialism. To strengthen the national will against foreign encroachment, he advocated the adoption of several basic principles as the basis for nation-building:

1. government as a civil rather than religious institution;
2. sectarianism as a divisive political and social force to be suppressed in civil society;
3. education as a necessity for a civil society.

Abduh considered these to be the essential characteristics of the Western nations, but not necessarily peculiar to them, for these same characteristics were legitimated within Islam.

To forestall the advance of Western imperialism, Abduh advocated the reform and renewal of the *Khalafah* in the framework of the Ottoman empire: 'Abduh considered Khalafah to be a de facto reality existing in political circumstances dominated by European imperial encroachment toward the East, the Muslim homeland. He had great hopes that this reality could be exploited to hinder imperialist expansion in these lands.'[4]

Rashid Redha was the most prominent and dedicated disciple of Muhammad 'Abduh. Born in Tripoli in 1865, he pursued religious studies and journalism in Syria until 1897, when he moved to Cairo. There he established a periodical, *al-Manar*, through which he disseminated, interpreted and elaborated on the ideas of Muhammad Abduh and others. Redha's main contribution to Islamic political thought was his dissemination of the ideas of al-Afghani and Abduh, the two foremost modernization reformers. He also championed the cause of the Wahhabi doctrine in his journal.

Despite their differing analyses and prescriptions, all of the Islamic modernization reformers confronted one or more of the four key issues on which the future of the Islamic world seemed to depend. Those issues were:

1. Morality, religious faith and development. To what extent did the external power and internal welfare of the Islamic world depend on the religious character and moral code of the *umma*?
2. Islam and scientific progress. What role did the lack of scientific progress play in Islamic weakness *vis-à-vis* Europe? How could this imbalance be redressed? Were modern technology and empirical scientific inquiry compatible with Islam?
3. Islam and political institutions. What political reforms were needed to strengthen the Islamic world? What political lessons could be learned from the West? To what degree was European experience applicable to, and compatible with, the political precepts of Islam?
4. Islam, nationalism and development. Did modern nationalism have a role to play in national development? To what degree was such nationalism compatible with Islam?

Islam, morality and development

The belief that a relationship existed between religious faith and community morality on the one hand, and the welfare and the advancement of the community on the other, was fundamental to Islam. It had been an accepted tenet of Islamic thought from the beginning, and was a concept inherent in the teachings of the Prophet himself. In fact, the Salafiyah movement was motivated by a belief that the *umma* was being harmed by immorality or deviation from the correct path of Islam.[5]

This belief continued to find expression in the works of the modernization reformers of the nineteenth and twentieth centuries. In many cases, however, it found expression in new terms and generated new prescriptions. The moral threat posed by European materialism and positivism, and the potential moral role that could be played by Islamic governments through education and example became prominent themes.

Al-Tahtawi was among those who stressed both of these themes. He asserted that social welfare was dependent upon both material well-being and 'the training of the character in religious and human virtues'.[6] Moreover, the former was dependent on the latter, such that the economic progress of a nation is dependent on its code of ethics. In turn, education provides the method for inculcating the appropriate virtues. Although al-Tahtawi was fascinated by European civilization, he was wary of the danger posed by European positivism. He warned that, in France, people believed that national welfare and human progress could take the place of religion.

Later, al-Afghani placed similar emphasis on the importance of morality and faith. His analysis stemmed from his assumption that 'whenever the cause for progress weakens, the result is backwardness and decadence, and whenever the reason for the fall is eliminated, the result is progress'.[7] The 'cause of progress', he asserted, was religion: 'religion was the foundation of all nations and the cause of their success'.[8] Human virtues – shame, trust, truthfulness – were essential to human happiness. The 'reason for the fall' was therefore the decline of religion and morality:

> the advent of materialism in Egypt and Persia in the guise of [Ismaili] batini propaganda, undermined the faith of the Muslim peoples by sowing the seeds of doubt in their minds and releasing their followers from religious or moral obligations, on the insidious ground that such obligations were prescribed for the uninitiated only. As the Muslims lost their moral stamina, they were so enfeebled that a small band of Franks were able to establish and maintain a firm foothold in their midst for two hundred years. Subsequently, the hordes of Genghis Khan were able to trample the whole band of Islam, sack its cities, and massacre its people.[9]

This process had reached its zenith with the intrusions of modern European imperialism. What was now required was a reformation and rebirth of Islam. 'A religious movement is essential because if we look for the reason for Europe's change from backwardness to civilization, we find it to be a religious movement since the days of Luther.'[10] Such a reformation necessitated in turn a revitalization of the *ulama*, the reopening of the gates of *ijtihad*, and other measures whereby Islam would be liberated from the materialism, traditionalism and stagnation which had afflicted it. Islamic unity – an end to the political and religious divisions which had plagued the *umma* since the death of the Prophet – was of fundamental importance. Al-Afghani suggested that all these reforms could be facilitated by the 'Arabization' of the Ottoman empire.

> The Turks ignored a great issue, and that is adopting the Arab tongue as the State's tongue. Had the Ottoman state taken the Arabic tongue as the official tongue, and attempted to Arabize the Turks, it would have acquired the utmost power. However, it did the opposite, it thought about Turkifying the Arabs, what a

nonsensical policy and ill opinion! Had it become Arabized the national difference between the two nations would have disappeared, together with the reasons of distaste and divisions, and they would have become one Arabic nation . . . .[11]

Islam, science and development

A second theme popular among Islamic modernization reformers was that of scientific and technological advancement, its role in Eastern and Western development, and its relationship with Islam. The urgency of this theme was, for many writers, underscored by Europe's relative scientific superiority, and the important role technology played in European economic and military penetration of the Islamic world.

Modern technology was of considerable interest to al-Tahtawi, and to him it seemed imperative that Egypt should adopt it. He noted that the European countries had 'reached the highest degree of perfection in the mathematical sciences, physics, and meta-physics', while the Islamic countries had 'perfected the legal [Shari'a] sciences and their application, and philosophy, but completely neglected the applied sciences in totality.'[12] The solution to this technological gap was to be found in promoting interaction with Europe and encouraging the immigration of foreign experts to Egypt.

Khayr al-Din also deplored the 'backwardness of the umma in [technological] skills'.[13] He was laudatory of trade fairs, the patent system, and other European mechanisms for stimulating innovation and technology, as well as of the French educational system. He was highly critical of those who opposed the importation of Western technology simply because it was from the West. He argued that not only had such technology often sprung from medieval Arab origins, but that, furthermore, the Prophet himself had not hesitated to use foreign technology where appropriate. Given this, 'what objection can there be today to our adopting certain skills that we see we greatly need in order to resist intrigues and attract benefits?'[14]

Ali Mubarak (1824–93) was another writer who took up this issue of European development versus Eastern backwardness. He observed that it was the 'spreading scope of science and information' that led Europe from its early 'state of barbarism and roughness' to its current success. Mubarak, however, also emphasized the indebtedness of the Europeans to the medieval Arab sciences upon which they had built. He argued that 'there is nothing in the teaching of religion [e.g. Islam] that prohibits progress in any useful science of life or religion, and that Islam was actually the reason behind the revival of the "old civilization" and what had perished of art and useful industries . . . .'[15] The decline of Islamic science was not due to any slackness or change in the nature of their laws or customs. Rather, the decline of Islamic science was the combined result of receding respect for science and scientists, and the deviation of the rulers of the *umma* from the benevolent path of their early Muslim predecessors. It was this respect among the early Muslims for science and knowledge that prompted its expansion, not only in the area of law and Arabic literature, but also with regard to agriculture, navigation, trade, medicine, mathematics and philosophy.

European assertions (made by Renan and others) that religion in general, and Islam in particular, were incompatible with modern scientific progress, provoked contrary responses from a number of Islamic writers. Al-Afghani, for example, responded to Renan by accepting that a conflict did exist between religion and scientific philosophy. Nevertheless, he also attempted to show that Islam subsumed all the rationality upon which modern scientific inquiry depended, and pointed to the achievements of the medieval Arab world as evidence of this. He argued that any apparent contradictions between scientific truth and Islam were actually due to rigid and inaccurate interpretations of the latter.

'Abduh also took up the challenge of Renan and his disciples. While Christianity may be incompatible with rational examination, he asserted, Islam is not. Rashid Redha went still further, arguing that Islam, by providing the necessary intellectual and moral characteristics, held the key to rapid technological progress. Moreover, acquiring elements of European science was an essential – albeit not *the* essential – factor in strengthening the *umma*.

Islam, political institutions and development

A third area of concern addressed by the reformers of the nineteenth and early twentieth centuries concerned the nature of government in modern Islamic societies. In the course of this discussion, two themes emerged as dominant. The first was revivalist in nature, advocating a return to the path set by the early Muslim rulers. The second draws its inspiration from Europe, and attempts to reconcile European and Islamic political philosophy.

Often, these two themes were synthesized into a single view of politics, and al-Tahtawi was one of the earliest writers to achieve such a synthesis, albeit a limited one. While accepting a traditional division of society into ruler and ruled, with the latter subject to the former and the former responsible to God, al-Tahtawi sought to institutionalize and delimit this relationship through constitutionalism. The legislative, judicial and executive functions of government must themselves be restrained by higher laws. The 'ruled' must be allowed to acquire freedom and public benefits, and their civil rights should be upheld.

The ruler should consult both the *ulama* and scientific specialists in the course of governing. Furthermore, he should be influenced by public opinion, and for this purpose all citizens should receive a political education adequate for them to understand the laws, rights and duties associated with citizenship.

Politico-administrative factors represented a central part of Khayr al-Din's analysis of European and Islamic civilization. He argued that European political reforms had set forth the basis for the advancement of European civilization by providing justice and freedom for all citizens. The core of these reforms had been the establishment of a legal-constitutional framework within which executive ministers were responsible for their actions to representative assemblies. He found an Islamic parallel to these institutions in the *Shari'a* (which acted as an overarching legal framework), and the process of consulting (*ahl al-hal wa al-'aqd*). It was the existence of these institutions during the golden age of Islamic civilization which had guaranteed power and prosperity. Khayr al-Din advocated that the ruler should consult the *ulama* and the notables (*a'yan*), and should act within the constraints of the *Shari'a*. This necessitated that the *'ulama'* be aware of modern developments. Khayr al-Din was a fervent supporter of reform (*tanzimat*) within the Ottoman empire, and a strong critic of its conservative opponents.

A Tunisian contemporary of Khayr al-Din, Ahmed-Bin-Abi al-Dhiyyaf (1806–76) also stressed political factors in his examination of Islamic society. In his *Ithaf Ahl al-Zaman bi Akhbar Muluk Tunis wa Ahd al-Aman*, al-Dhiyyaf identified three types of rule (*mulk*): autocratic, republican and nomocratic. Of these, the first is the least preferable, since autocracy leads to tyranny and exploitation, and destroys human virtues so that .

> some Muslims in different parts have come to be slaves of taxes, with nothing of their homeland and country and the origin of their fathers and grandfathers, except giving out Dirhams and Dinars humiliatingly and disgracefully . . . until they renounced love of country (watan) and home, and abandoned the morals of

a free man. This is the major reason for the weakening and destruction of the Islamic kingdoms.[16]

Absolute rule is unjust rule, and 'the injustice of the rulers is the most powerful reason behind the destruction of states . . . .'[17]

Al-Dhiyyaf admitted that Republican rule, as practised in the United States, had brought benefits to its citizens. He rejected it on Islamic grounds, however, arguing that guidance of the *umma* is the essence of Islam and cannot be left to temporal needs alone. Instead, he advocated a system of government wherein the ruler would be guided by reason and law. Should he violate these constraints, his subjects would be released from their oath of loyalty (*bay'a*).

Islam, nationalism and development

A fourth feature apparent in the writings of many Islamic modernization reformers concerned the role of nationalism and its place in development. European nation-state centred conceptions of national identification were relatively new to an Islamic world which had historically been united (or divided) by the transcendent appeal of Islam itself. Al-Tahtawi was one of the earliest nineteenth-century reformers to explicitly expound the virtues of nationalism. For him, Egypt – rather than the Arab world or the Ottoman empire – was the focus of national aspiration. He considered that citizenship implied duties, as well as rights, on the part of all within the nation. He stressed that patriotism transcended the ties of religion, so that

all that is binding on a believer in regard to his fellow believers is binding also on members of the same watan in their mutual rights. For there is a national brotherhood between them over and above the brotherhood in religion. There is a moral obligation on those who share the same watan to work together to improve it and perfect its organization in all that concerns its honour and greatness and wealth.[18]

The fundamental centrality of Islamic unity and pan-Islamic co-operation in the works of al-Afghani and 'Abduh reduced nationalism to a secondary element. They regarded the Islamic *umma* as a superior basis for cohesion and commitment to European nationalism. Indeed, they considered European nationalism – based as it was on cultural and racial homogeneities – as an essentially divisive force. The Islamic community, on the other hand, was based on a moral commitment that protected all members – even non-Muslims. *Al-Urwa al-Wothga,* the influential Paris-based journal edited by al-Afghani and Abduh observed that religion 'is the strongest bond that unites the Arab and the Turk, the Persian and the Indian, the Egyptian and the Moroccan.'[19]

The Westernization problem

Internal and external pressures for the 'Westernization' of the Islamic world continued to build up during the first half of the twentieth century, and became particularly acute in the period between the First and Second World Wars. Many Arab intellectuals, having received their educations in Europe, returned to their native countries advocating the emulation of European civilization as a cure for the poverty and underdevelopment of the Islamic world. Such a call for Westernization generally assumed one or more of three basic positions:

1. Westernization in the broadest sense of the term, whereby the advancement of the East was sought through copying the social, political, economic and technological institutions and structures of the West. This trend was represented by Egyptian intellectuals such as Ahmad Lufti al-Sayyed, Salama Mussa, Taha Hussein and Mahmoud Azmi, all of whom advocated the concept of 'Egyptian or Pharaonic nationalism' which explicitly rejected any Arab, Islamic or Eastern orientation.
2. Liberalism, which implied that minds should be liberated from the bondage of preconceived beliefs and traditions in order to examine empirically and independently all issues relevant to knowledge and society. This approach was followed by Taha Hussein, who adopted the Cartesian method, and by Salama Mussa and Ismael Madhar who related scientific liberalism to the Darwinian theories of evolution.
3. Secularism. This trend called for a constitution based on civil law and the establishment of a state on 'modern Western foundations' in which religion would be separated from the state. This was actually implemented in Turkey by Kamal Attaturk in 1924. However, by 1925 this idea came to be strongly associated with Sheikh Ali Abd Al-Raziq. It was this aspect of Westernization more than any other that spurred the development of Islamic political thought during the inter-war period.

In many cases the advocacy of such measures by Westernized Arab intellectuals was accompanied by an explicit or implicit devaluation of their own (Arab, Islamic) cultural heritage. In part, this devaluation stemmed from a tendency to contrast the poverty of Arab societies with an idealized view of the achievements of European civilization, which glossed over the latter's shortcomings. More significantly, however, calls for Westernization reflected the political and military defeats of the Arab world, which had led to a willingness on the part of the conquered to emulate their conquerors (a general phenomenon noted by Ibn Khaldun over five centuries earlier). The stagnation of the *ulama* – who, more often than not, were afflicted by a rigidity and traditionalism which rendered them virtual prisoners of the past, unable to cope with the new circumstances of the nineteenth and twentieth centuries – only served to reinforce these trends.

The tide of Westernization, however, did not go unchecked. Muhammad Rashid Redha and Moheb al-Din al-Khateb were both religious writers who, while well aware of the benefits that could come from the West, strongly opposed the liberal-secular attack on Islamic and Arab culture. Other thinkers, such as Mansoor Fahmy, Muhammad Kurd Ali, Muhammad Hussein Heikal and Ismael Madhar – many of whom were originally secular and Westernized – revised their initial positions and turned instead to defending Islamic culture.

Mansoor Fahmy, for example, strongly criticized Taha Hussein for what he saw as a blind commitment to Westernization:

> There is a big difference between he who takes from others and uses their means, and he who takes from others in order to depend on them, thus limiting his own potentialities and intrinsic activity. There is a great difference between he who takes the weapons of others in order to conquer them, and he who takes their weapons to be their guide . . . . Don't those who call and ask us to fully follow the Westerners in culture and other fields, see that they actually call for accepting servitude and to being led?[20]

Fahmy emphasized that there existed fundamental differences between the Arab world and the West in terms of traditions, history and circumstances – differences which rendered the systems and institutions of the West wholly inappropriate. Moreover, the heritage of the Arab world was both God-given and an essential part of national dignity, and therefore should not be discarded:

My soul calls upon me to preserve the characteristics that God wanted to characterize a nation which I am from; and to adhere to a heritage that came down to my country centuries ago, and to be inspired by what my history inspires. A nation that demands its dignity has to be different from other nations in characteristics and features.[21]

For his part, Muhammad Hussain Heikal (1924–c.1980), a distinguished Egyptian author and statesman, saw the devaluation of the Arab world's Islamic heritage as part of European efforts to encourage dependence on the West and thereby facilitate political domination. He argued that, while the West had a great intellectual contribution to make to the resurgence of the East, the latter's spiritual inspiration should be sought closer to home in Islam. Writing in 1933 as the chief editor of the newspaper *al-Siyassa*, Heikal described the intellectual process which led him to adopt this position:

I have tried to transfer to those who speak my language the moral and spiritual culture of the West in order that we would take it as a guide and a light for us. However, I came to recognize after a while that I am planting the seed where it cannot grow . . . and no life came to it. I then turned to seek in our deep history of the Pharaohs a source of inspiration for this era in which it would grow a new growth. However, I found that time and mental stagnation have cut all ties between us and that time which could provide a seed for a new revival. I searched again and saw that our Islamic history is the only seed which grows and fruits. There is no escape therefore except to return to our history in order to seek the foundations of the moral life in order to avoid the danger that the nationalist ideas forced the West into.[22]

This view that Islam and Arabism should provide the spiritual basis for Eastern resurgence was echoed by a number of other thinkers. Ismael Madhar (1891–1962), an Egyptian scholar, emphasized that 'every Arab should be from the inside an Arab in soul and spirit, with his example being the morals of the Arabs and Islam.'[23]

Muhammad Kurd Ali (1876–1953), a Syrian journalist and scholar, conceptualized the Westernization problem in terms of a contest between 'old' and 'new', a conflict which the latter seemed to be winning. In doing so, however, the supporters of the 'new' had embraced European enlightenment at the expense of Islamic teachings.

If you ask them about what is allowed and what is forbidden, and what religions have decreed, they would arrogantly tell you that the nation lives by its 'new' and not by its 'old', and that this 'old' if it doesn't hurt us taking it, would at least not benefit us; the sane should only take what is good for him and that which elevates him.[24]

Kurd Ali noted that between the two extremes of old and new existed a third group who advocated 'not throwing away the "old" in its totality or taking the "new" as a whole. Instead choose to take what is useful in everything'.[25] He himself supported this approach, and emphasized that while 'there is no solution to our conditions without taking from the European civilization' it must also be recognized by the supporters of the 'new' that 'this new civilization that has dazzled them by its decorations and accoutrements will not benefit them over their fellow men unless accompanied by the knowledge of our predecessors and their tradition'.[26] In other words, Kurd Ali called for a synthesis of Western and Arab knowledge within a context of intellectual freedom.

Islam and the state

As noted earlier, the Westernization problem –although having broad repercussions on virtually all aspects of Islamic thought during this period – had its greatest political ramifications with regard to the question of religion's appropriate relationship with the modern state. Advocates of secularization asserted that the interference of religion in the affairs of the state had the effect of slowing development, and that while such interference may have once been tolerable, it was no longer tolerable in contemporary societies. What was needed, they argued, was the replacement of Islamic law with western civil law, and the relegation of Islam to a spiritual system of ontological beliefs about God, man and the hereafter, stripped of its social and political dimensions.

Initially, many of the advocates of secularization were non-Arabs and non-Muslims. A few Egyptians also supported these ideas, such as Mahmoud Azmi of the Democratic Party (and later the Liberal-Constitutional Party) who in 1922 attacked Islamic legal jurisdiction and Islam's constitutional status as Egypt's official religion in articles in the newspapers *al-Ahram* and *al-Istiqlal*. Nevertheless, such ideas would have had only a limited impact if it had not been for Ali Abd al-Razik, an al-Azhar-educated religious scholar and judge, who wrote a work on Islamic political authority in 1925 which not only supported such ideas but even attempted to prove – both from the Qur'ān and history – that Islam itself called for them.[27]

Arguing that the *Khalafah* had no foundation in the Qur'ān, the Sunna or Hadith, al-Razik maintained that Islam never decided a particular form of government, and that the Muslims were never required to follow a particular system. The *Khalafah* was never a religious system, and the Qur'ān did not allude to it or order it. In fact, the *Khalafah* had paralysed development in the form of government among Muslims. He even maintained that the Prophet did not have the intention of forming a government or establishing a state. The *Khalafah* in Islam, Abd al-Razik contended, was 'based on nothing but brutal force.'[28] The virtue of Muslims does not depend on the *Khalafah* which was 'a catastrophe that hit Islam and the Muslims and is a source of evil and corruption.'[29] Therefore, the Muslims are free to choose their own form of government.

Abd al-Razik's major problem in putting forward this position was his inability to say what he really wanted to. At the time he published his book, the Sultan of Egypt was attempting to bestow on himself the title of Khalife – a position which was then vacant due to the abolition of the Ottoman *Khalafah* – in order to protect and legitimize his rule. Being unable to explicitly state that the characteristics necessary for a Khalife did not apply to the Sultan, Abd al-Razik opposed the move indirectly by attacking the institution of the *Khalafah* and the tradition of Islamic scholarship which supported it, rather than the Sultan himself. In doing so, however, he provoked a storm of opposition from orthodox Islamic scholars, whose harsh criticisms of his work eventually forced Abd al-Razik from public life.

Nevertheless, Abd al-Razik had a significant impact on contemporary Islamic thought by serving to stimulate new approaches to the problems of government in Islam. Among many thinkers the idea of the *Khalafah* was dropped in favour of a democratic Islamic government. This attitude was represented by several legal and political thinkers, such as Abd al-Hamid Ibn Badis of Algeria, Abd al-Raziq al-Sunhouri, Hasan al-Banna and Abd al-Qadir Audah of Egypt, Abd al-Rahman al-Bazzaz in Iraq and Alal al-Fasi in Morocco.

Abd al-Hamid Ibn Badis (1889–1940), the founder of the Algerian Society of Muslim Ulammas in 1931, was among the first to criticize the Ottoman *Khalafah* and the call on behalf of some al-Azhar scholars to bestow the title on the Sultan of Egypt. He maintained that the *Khalafah* had become 'a superficial symbol that had nothing to do with

Islam.'[30] Responding to the Sultan's attempts to become Khalife, Ibn Badis wrote 'enough conceit and trickery! The Islamic nations today – even the enslaved ones – are no longer fooled by such illusions', and concluded that 'the illusion of the Khalafah shall never be achieved and the Muslims someday – by God's Will – shall arrive to this opinion.'[31] Ibn Badis proposed in one of his articles a system of government which he based on Abu Bakr's speech based upon the thirteen principles:[32]

1. No one has the right to govern the nation except by its appointment and consent. The Umma has the right and power to appointment and removal.
2. He who takes over such a responsibility should be the most efficient not the best behaved.
3. He who takes over the government should not be considered better than the people of his Umma except by his deeds and performance.
4. The Umma has the right to supervise the rulers, since it is the source of their power.
5. The ruler has the right to demand support from his people as long as he is just.
6. The ruler has the right to be well advised by his people.
7. The Umma has the right to question and hold the rulers accountable for what they do. The rulers should also follow the will of the Umma.
8. He who rules the Umma should provide his programme or plan in order that it may be aware of what he is doing.
9. The Umma should not be ruled except by the law that it accepts for itself. The rulers are only implementors of the will of the Umma. Liberty and sovereignty are thus the right of every individual.
10. All people are equal before the law with no difference between the powerful and the weak.
11. All rights of all people are to be preserved irrespective of their power or weakness.
12. Balance should be maintained between the classes of the Umma. Rights are to be taken from the rich and given to the poor without being harsh or doing injustice to either.
13. There should be common feeling between the rulers and the ruled regarding their responsibility towards each other and towards society, always doing their best to improve its conditions, and aware that God is watching them.

Ibn Badis, however, never thought that the backwardness of the Muslims was due to any inherent weakness in the *Khalafah* system but to their abandonment of the cause of progress. 'The causes of life, civilization and progress are provided to all of mankind alike. He who follows a cause – with God's Will – shall reach his goal whether he is benevolent or sinister, a believer or a non-believer.'[33]

Another religious scholar who saw the *Khalafah* as a relatively unimportant side issue on the road to Islamic government was Hassan al-Banna (1906–49), founder of the Society of Moslem Brothers in Egypt in the late 1920s. Since al-Banna's contribution to Islamic political thought will be more fully explored in the next chapter, it will suffice here to summarize the principles which al-Banna saw as forming the basis of Islamic government:

1. The Ruler's responsibility: the government should be responsible before God and to the people. The ruler is only a servant of the Umma based on a just 'social contract'.
2. The Umma's unity: within the framework of 'brotherhood' among its members, without which the complete meaning of Islam is not achieved – a spiritual and social unity.
3. The respect of the will of the Umma: it is the right of the Umma to supervise closely its ruler, and advise him as to the path that he should follow and the general benefits that it seeks. The ruler on his part is responsible to respect its will and follow its opinion.[34]

According to al-Banna, such principles can be observed and practised by a representative assembly. Although this institution is often perceived as having come from the West, al-Banna saw no objection to making use of it: 'there is nothing in the principles of the representative system that contradicts with the principles that Islam had laid for the government system.'[35] Al-Banna's model of Islamic government thus closely approached the democratic system of the West, accepting the representative system. The ruler is not a Khalife but simply a person who is responsible to his *umma* and people.

Another man who called strongly for the combination of state and religion and emphasized the compatibility of the Islamic laws with the conditions of progress and advancement was Abd al-Aziz Gawish (1876–1929), an Egyptian journalist and scholar; he raised the slogan 'Islam is suitable for all times and all places', since it was the religion of individualism and freedom. He also identified several basic principles which should be considered in applying the law, such as *ijtihad*, public interest, equality among Muslims and non-Muslims before the law. He believed that if these rules were honestly and freely adhered to, beneficial results could be expected from the application of the *Shari'a* at any time and in any place.

For Abd al-Raham al-Bazzaz (1913–73), an Iraqi jurist and statesman, a major danger to Islam was innovation, resulting from contamination with outside ideas. The most dangerous of these ideas was the secularization of social and political life:

> Islam rejects this idea staunchly. It bases its beliefs, arranges its systems and spreads its philosophy on a consolidated basis of unity of life; that is it does not approve of dividing our life between this life [on earth] and our other life which we expect. Those two lives are amalgamated and tied together to the fullest extent. The one [life on earth] is the path to the other [life after death], and the legal principles include both equally: thus it is not possible to divide life in the true Islamic perspective between a mundane life organized by specified objective principles which have no relation to religion, and another organized by a religion that has no relation to the state . . . . There isn't in Islam Christ and Caesar, or church and state.[36]

Al-Bazzaz attacked those who called for the adoption of a Western legal code by arguing that laws are central to, and reflective of, the social and moral life of a nation and are therefore not transportable. Moreover, he attempted to show that the *Shari'a* is superior to Western legal systems because: (1) it combines law with religion, morality and justice; (2) it emphasizes the priority of the community; (3) it amalgamates rights and duties; (4) it is dynamic and adaptable. He called for the revitalization of the Arab world, not through the re-establishment of the *Khalafah*, but rather through the establishment of an Islamic state: 'an Islamic state with no priesthood, socialistic but far from the excesses of communism, consultative but free from democratic hypocrisy, free but far from anarchy, with people free in the way their mothers gave them birth, equal like the teeth of a comb, not having privileges over others except by piety.'[37] Like al-Banna, al-Bazzaz believed that such reform could only be achieved through the foundation of a party or a grouping which 'honestly believes in Islam, recognizes its truth perfectly, and functions by the means of the age and its ways, honestly and sincerely to achieve its goals and ideals, without hesitation or fear.'[38]

Abd al-Qadir Audah (d.1955), a leading Muslim Brotherhood theoretician and jurist, was also concerned with the issue of Islamic law versus civil law and in 1945 he studied the *Shari'a* in order to compare it with the civil law in general and Western criminal law in particular. He came to the conclusion that the Islamic law was superior to Western legal codes. He identified several points in which the *Shari'a* was different from civil law:

1. Civil law was a creation of human beings, while the Shari'a was a creation of God. As such, civil law is liable to be changed with time, whereas the Shari'a does not change with time or place.
2. Civil law is a group of temporary principles set by the community in order to organize and meet its demands. In this sense it lags behind the community, since laws do not change as fast as a community does. It is also temporary in the same sense. The Shari'a, on the other hand, is based upon principles laid down by God to permanently organize the communities; this requires that its principles and texts be flexible and general in order to meet the demands of the people, irrespective of time or change of demands.
3. It is the community that makes civil law, whereas the Shari'a makes the community by creating healthy individuals and an ideal society.

Thus, the *Shari'a* is superior to civil law in three respects: it is perfect, supreme and permanent.

Audah also discussed the problems of dictatorship and democracy, and Islam's ability to combine the virtues of both systems. The Islamic ruler, he argued, owed his position to a social contract with the people, was responsible for his deeds and misdeeds, and was liable to be deposed if he wielded his power unjustly. The power of the ruler should be limited, and exercised for the good of the community as a whole. Audah concluded that the Islamic world's backwardness was attributable to its failure to implement the *Shari'a*:

> the reason behind our backwardness and decadence is that we did not apply the Shari'a justly nor fully during our late dark periods. Our Turkish and Mameluke leaders followed their desires in everything they cared for and applied the Shari'a where it did not harm nor benefit them. If the reason behind our backwardness

is our neglect of the Shari'a and the abandonment of its laws, it shall serve as no good to take [other] laws, and instead it will accelerate our backwardness and decadence more and more. Our infallible remedy is to eliminate the cause of backwardness and return to the laws of the Shari'a.[39]

Another scholar-statesman who examined the issue of progress and democracy in the Islamic world was 'Alal al-Fasi (1910–74), leader of the Moroccan Independence Party. In order for democracy – or, as al-Fasi puts it, 'the general thought' – to function properly, it has to depend on the opinion of the vast majority of the nation, which at the same time has to be enlightened and freed from superstitious and corrupt traditions. Enlightened public opinion was of the utmost importance in leading to progress, and al-Fasi gave it priority over all other social factors.

Al-Fasi, however, identified several conditions which must prevail if an ideology appropriate for influencing and directing public opinion is to be established:

1. The ideology has to be functional to the existence of the nation and its forward progress.
2. It should meet the demands and requirements of the nation.
3. Progressiveness, that is, directing the nation towards the ideals which it determines as a goal.
4. Comprehensiveness, that is, the ideology should consider all aspects of life and promote their progress.

What then is the ideal that a nation should pursue? Al-Fasi identifies such an ideal as 'pleasing Him who has our fate in his hands [i.e. God] and reaching paradise in the highest of heavens.' In other words, 'all our works, orientations, programmes, and principles should be directed towards the achievement of the Divine Will regarding the construction of earth and its reform, maintaining brotherhood among its people, and exploring what fate has provided us with of means to achieve our happiness in life.'[40]

Al-Fasi thus rejected the separation of religion from social life, and the *Shari'a* from the rules of this life. He also completely rejected the 'new Israelite ideas' which appeared in the words of Ali Abd al-Razik when the latter claimed that 'Islam is void of the principles of government and that the prophet was only a religious and moral preacher who did not interfere in the affairs of the state or its construction.'[41] Al-Fasi argued that the idea of separating church from state was actually a principle of Christianity rather than a revolt against it resulting from the historical development of Christian Churches in Europe. Moreover, the revolt of Western Europe against the Church was a result of the latter's support of the feudal system.

> If Islamic history never needed to form such a theory, it was because the power of the church never existed in Islam at all, and power in all issues belongs to the people. What the Moslems see as good, is good in the sight of God. Had Islam been persecuted in its history as Christianity, its followers would have needed to adopt such a theory that is strange to them. However, they did not understand Islam except when it was a judge over others and in control of the rulers.[42]

Thus, the *Shari'a* cannot be separated from social life because it is associated with the ideal of 'establishing the divine will of constructing the earth and maintaining justice among its people.'[43] Since justice is what the *Shari'a* seeks, it is inevitable that the judicial system should be 'a principal part of Islam, and the courts and laws in the state are called upon to be based on the laws of the Shari'a.'[44] Unlike civil laws based on the will of the strongest, the *Shari'a* represented a divinely-inspired blueprint for societal order and the achievement of the highest human ideals.[45]

Islam and socialism

In contrast to Europe, where socialist ideas had been generated and acted upon amid the immediate material pressures of rapid industrialization, many Arab and Muslim thinkers first encountered socialist ideology at an intellectual level, as a result of observing or being educated in the West. As a consequence, their analyses of socialism were largely theoretical in nature. It was not until a relatively late period, during the 1940s, that domestic industrialization, the growing international stature of the USSR, and the expanding appeal of socialist and communist groups in the Arab East, forced Islamic thinkers to confront socio-economic issues and the question of socialism as a matter of some urgency. This urgency became still greater in the 1950s, with the ascendance of progressive governments in Egypt and other Arab countries, and with the expansion of Soviet influence in the region.

One response to the challenge of socialist ideology in the Islamic world was to assert its superfluity by claiming that Islam already subsumed all its positive features. Typical of this response was Amir Shakib Arsalan (1969–1946), a Lebanese scholar-statesman. During the inter-war period he insisted that 'in the Islamic Shari'a there are great socialist principles'[46] which, due to their divine origin, are far superior to the socialist ideas of Europe. Arsalan perceived the *Zakat*, or alms, as the most important Islamic socialist base and emphasized the fact that 'if Muslims gave out the Zakat lawfully, and offered one tenth of their agricultural produce, two and a half percent of their money, and one out of forty of their animals, or as stated in the legal (Fiqh) books, there would remain not even one Muslim who may be called poor'.[47] He then attacked those Muslims who advocate a socialist system that calls for 'conflict and the outbreak of class wars like the wars taking place in Europe and America.'[48] Arsalan thus insisted that there is no .

> shield to protect Islamic society from this inevitable tribulation except by imposing Zakat in the legal sense, provided that there is a ministry or department in every Islamic government that organizes its collection and the means of its spending such that if socialism enters the Islamic countries, it would do so without noise or conflict, but instead become a cause for reviving one of the most sacred religious imperatives, namely Zakat.[49]

Another Muslim thinker who concerned himself with the socio-economic problems of contemporary Islam was Abd al-Rahman al-Bazzaz, who discussed socialism within the context of what he called the 'communal inclination' in Islam. He argued that the two main orientations which divide people among different ideologies and philosophies are those of the 'individualistic orientation' and the 'collectivist orientation'. The former goes to a great length to design laws and institutions which serve the individual and his desires, which thereby lead to selfishness, economic chaos and social decadence. The latter, on the other hand, excessively interferes in the affairs of the individual, depriving him of free will. Islam, however, by recognizing individualism and individual rights within the general framework of its 'communal inclination', represents an ideal philosophy capable of harmonizing these two orientations. Al-Bazzaz cited group prayers, pilgrimage, *Zakat*, and calls for justice, mercy and sincerity as examples of Islamic forms of behaviour in the general interest of the society or community.

Whereas Arsalan and al-Bazzaz primarily reacted to socialist ideology by stressing Islam's community emphasis, other Muslim thinkers made more detailed attempts to elucidate socio-economic guidelines from Islam. For Abd al-Qadir Audah, the starting point for such analysis was God's ultimate ownership of all wealth. Drawing his inspiration from the Qur'ān, Audah stated that 'all property belongs to God and people only have the right to use it.'[50] Thus, God did not create it for any one individual or group of people. Everything that human beings acquire is therefore lent them by God, and they have no real ultimate right of ownership. As for the Qur'ānic verses which attribute property to man (for example 'give to the orphans their property', *Surah* IV:2), they do not indicate ownership, but indicate instead that some individuals had 'acquired the right to use it'.[51] Acquired wealth is then to be used for investment (such as in agriculture or mining), spent on basic needs, or transferred by inheritance, trade or donations. Although these are legitimate sources of expenditure, they should nevertheless be used 'reasonably, without lavishness or stinginess.'[52]

Many implications arise from the fact that 'all money belongs to God'. No human being has the right to absolute property ownership. The community, through its ruler and representatives, has the right to organize the economic system within which wealth is used, to limit the individual acquisition of wealth, and to confiscate wealth for the general good, provided that adequate compensation is given. The individual too has certain rights: the right to acquire and transfer property, the right to permanent ownership, and the right to enjoy the benefits of ownership provided that indirect benefits flow to the community therefrom.

At the same time as identifying the rights of the individual and the community, Islam also imposes duties on its followers. The first of these is *Zakat*, one of the five pillars of Islam. The second obligation, which is required when *Zakat* is inadequate to meet the needs of the community, is public expenditure to meet these needs. Audah states that, in any event, an Islamic government may always 'take away from the surplus money of the rich and give to the poor, even if the latter did not need it, if the general interest required that.'[53]

A more extensive elucidation of Islam as a comprehensive socio-economic doctrine was provided at about the same time by a Muslim Brotherhood thinker, Sayyid Qutb (1906–66), in his work *al-Adalat Ijtima'iyah fi al-Islam*. For Qutb, Islam provided a form of social justice which was 'a comprehensive human justice, and not merely an economic justice',[54] a justice within which material, spiritual, and moral values are completely unified. It is in this latter respect that Islam diverges from communism on one hand and Christianity on the other, by providing the spiritual values absent in the former and the material necessities absent in the latter.

According to Qutb, Islamic social justice does not require equal pay and the abolition of class differences, since it allows individuals to gain from their mental and physical endowments and achieve 'pre-eminence through hard work'.[55] Instead, Islam calls for equality of opportunity while recognizing the 'fundamental equality' of all men.

Qutb considered three basic principles on which Islam builds its concept of social justice, namely: (1) absolute spiritual freedom; (2) total human equality; (3) strong social co-operation:

1. Spiritual freedom: such freedom releases the hidden forces in human beings, causing them to transcend their humiliating subservience to necessities. When Islam liberated human conscience it liberated man from all forms of servitude except to God, eliminating any master/slave relationships among human beings. Such feelings also liberate men from fear of the future, fear for the security of wealth and fear for the security of social status since all this in the hands of God. This is not to say that people should not seek material goods; on the contrary, Qutb recognizes that material survival is essential and that the 'empty belly cannot appreciate high-sounding phrases'.[56] This situation is dealt with in Islam by requiring both wealthy individuals and the state to provide social assistance as a religious obligation, the neglect of which is punishable in both this world and the hereafter.

2. Human equality: which is a natural outcome of spiritual freedom. Islam emphasized the unity of human kind in origin, destiny, rights and duties, and called upon all people to come together and ignore tribal, racial and religious prejudices. It also decreed equality between men and women except when one sex was more capable of performing a particular job than the other.

3. Social co-operation: Islam has determined that the interest of society is of top priority, and related individual freedom and human equality to this priority. In return for individual rights, Islam imposed both individual and social duties on both

individuals and the community. Because of these duties, the state has the right to take money from the rich and give it to the poor in order to meet the latter's demands.

What then are the practical means by which social justice could be attained? According to Qutb, this kind of justice in Islam evolves from 'the human conscience' and from 'within the soul'. In other words, Islamic social justice is not merely economic justice, but rather a combination of conscience and law. This combination is best exemplified by the *Zakat* system, which is not only a duty imposed and administered by the state, but also a religious obligation whose omission is a sin.

In more practical terms, however, Qutb presented his idea of social justice within the context of an Islamic economic policy concerning private ownership and the means of acquisition and expenditure. Qutb starts by emphasizing that private ownership is undoubtedly a right that is approved by Islam. Any attack on private property is completely prohibited and severely punishable. This right also includes inheritance. However, Qutb indicates that such a right should not be exercised at the expense of the interest of the community. Accordingly, Islam imposes so many restrictions on ownership that it almost becomes a theoretical rather than a practical right. Qutb identified a number of Islamic principles regarding private ownership:

1. 'the individual is in a way a steward of his property on behalf of society; his tenure of property is a form of salary which is greater than the actual right of possession. Property in the widest sense is a right which can only belong to society, which in turn receives it as a trust from Allah who is the only true owner of anything'.[57] In other words, property rights in Islam are subordinated to the public interest. If an individual does not act responsibly, the community has the right to remove that right from the individual.
2. Wealth should not be monopolized in the hands of any one group of people since this would create a social imbalance which may give rise to prejudices and hatred among the members of the community.
3. Certain types of communal property, such as water, grazing, food and fuel are the absolute right of the community and no individual has the right to control them. The *Zakat* is also the right of the community.

Although Qutb repeatedly emphasized the important role that *Zakat* plays in community welfare, he also argued that it is not the only claim that the requirements of Islamic social justice can make on property. Indeed, he levelled sharp criticism at those *ulama* who seek to restrict the scope of such justice by claiming that *Zakat* represents 'the extreme limits of the demands which Islam can regularly make on capital':

> ... in fact the poor-tax is the lowest limit of the statutory duties on property, and it stands alone only when society does not require any additional income. But when the poor-tax is not enough, Islam need not feel that its hands are tied; on the contrary, it gives to the head of the administration wide powers to assign levies on capital – that is to say, forced contribution from capital at a reasonable rate – subject always to the permanent limitations of its own welfare.[58]

The tendency of many *ulama* to oppose socio-economic reforms, and their close connections with the Arab upper classes, led Egyptian religious scholar-statesman, Khaled Muhammad Khaled, to make similar charges in his work *Min Huna Nabd'a* in 1950. Khaled, angered by what he perceived to be an inclination on the part of al-Azhar scholars to ignore the needs of the poor and support unjust social systems, attacked their concepts of 'lovable poverty' and the 'socialism of charity'.[59]

The socialization and nationalization of the Egyptian economy during the 1950s, and the extension of such reforms to Syria after the formation of the United Arab Republic in 1958, intensified the debate over Islam and socialism. It was in this context that Mustafa al-Siba'i (1915–64), founder and leader of the Syrian branch of the Muslim Brotherhood, wrote *Ishtra Kiyat al-Islam*.[60] This book caused an uproar, not so much because of its content, but rather because of its title, which explicitly associated socialism with Islam.

Al-Siba'i's motive for writing this book was basically to discredit Nasser's socialist policies. He maintained that socialism is an inclination which all people, particularly in the underdeveloped nations, strive to attain in order to rid themselves of the burden of social injustice and class inequalities. The basic goal of socialism is to prevent any individual from exploiting capital in order to become richer at the expense of the people. This is achieved through state supervision of the economic activity of the individual so that social co-operation among citizens is maintained and causes of poverty are eliminated. According to Siba'i, this is the identical goal of Islamic laws.

Al-Siba'i's central thesis was that the solution to poverty and the eradication of class differences cannot be achieved purely through nationalization. Instead, Islamic socialism is required. According to al-Siba'i, Islamic socialism is based on the recognition of five natural rights: the right to life, the right to freedom, the right to knowledge, the right to dignity, and the right of ownership. Recognizing that it is this latter right which causes most socio-economic disputes, al-Siba'i approached it in a similar way to Audah and Qutb, by emphasizing that God is the ultimate owner of all, and that man is deputized on behalf of God to use property. Work is the most important source of ownership. The state has the right to place some restrictions on wealth (through *Zakat*, the inheritance system, and limitations on the size of wealth), and to nationalize certain 'necessary goods' in the community interest.

Islamic socialism also entails laws regarding social co-operation, such as assisting the poor, the sick and the bankrupt; compensating the victims of serious accidents; and helping young people to get married. Al-Siba'i then identifies four factors which persuade people to adhere to such laws. The first of these is faith that there is a God who created this universe, who observes the works of man, who punishes or rewards him according to his deeds. The second factor is morality, which calls for generosity, co-operation, responsibility, and the enjoyment of good and prohibition of evil. The third factor is material in nature, involving punishment of those persons who violate the common good. The fourth factor identified by al-Siba'i is the law, drawn primarily from the Qur'ān and the Sunna.

Al-Siba'i's general view of socio-economic matters under Islam was more developed than Qutb's, in the two key areas of nationalization and land reform. Al-Siba'i clearly accepted nationalization as one of the measures which Islam recognized. Al-Siba'i did not, however, approve the principle of nationalization without restrictions. He suggested that 'the state should not resort to nationalizing industry or any other public utility except after taking the opinion of the economic and social experts'[61] who could determine the benefit or cost of such a procedure. As to those who indicate that deprivation of ownership should only take place by consent, Siba'i stressed that this need not be so since the Prophet and Khalifes had taken away land from owners without their consent. However, Siba'i emphasized again that 'if the state resorts to nationalization for a social necessity it has to compensate those whose ownership has been taken away in a just manner if their ownership of that wealth derived from legitimate means.'[62] Siba'i also did not hesitate to support land reform and the rights given to the workers who should be well paid and secured.

Such an Islamic system, al-Siba'i argued, avoids the shortcomings of capitalism, since 'Western capitalism is covered with the blood of the people'. As such, 'there is no compatibility between Islamic socialism and capitalism in any sphere, not in its economic belief nor its political reality.'[63] On the other hand, the Islamic system avoids the shortcomings of communism, whose theoretical views strip man of his spirit by reducing him to a selfish pursuer of economic interest and whose practical precepts call for bloody class struggle.

Although al-Siba'i was, as noted above, critical of Egyptian socialism, other Islamic writers held a different view. Prominent among these was Sheikh Mahmud Shaltut, a progressive religious scholar who served as the rector of al-Alzhar during the late 1950s and 1960s. Shaltut used Qur'anic citation to argue that socialism as practised in Nasser's Egypt was in conformity with Islam, and that intervention by the state in the social and economic spheres was necessary for the well-being and independence of the *umma*. According to Shaltut,

> agriculture, commerce and industry are the pillars of the national economy in all nations that wish to live an independent, enlightened, and worthy life. These three realms of activity must be coordinated so that the nation can reach the aim which Islam has assigned to it with the sole aim of preserving its existence and its governmental and administrative independence.

Because of this, Shaltut argued that it was vital that:

> Whoever holds authority in the Muslim community and influences its interests must therefore take steps to see to it that the nation draws the greatest profit possible from agriculture, commerce, and industry by coordinating the three sectors of activity so that, in the matter of investment, one does not develop at the expense of the others – even if this means transforming agricultural land into capital or industrial concerns, according to the country's needs as dictated by its interests.[64]

Shaltut concluded that 'government is therefore an organization that benefits the country and preserves it from all foreign interference.'

Notes

1. Muhammad Umarah (ed.), *al-'Amal al-Kamilah Rifa'a al-Tahtawi*, 2, Beirut, al-Mu'asasah al-Arabiyah lil Dirasat wa al-Nashir, 1973, p. 11.
2. Khayr al-Din al-Tunisi, *The Surest Path*, trans. Leon Carl Brown, Cambridge, Mass., Harvard University Press, 1967, p. 74.
3. Quoted in Ahmed Amin, *Zuma al-Islah fi al-Asir al-Hadith*, Beirut, Dar al-Kitab al-Arabi, n.d., p. 114.
4. Muhammad 'Umarah, *al-'Amal al-Kamilah lil Imam Muhammad Abduh*, 1, Beirut, al-Mu'asasah al-Arabiyah lil Dirasat wa al-Nashir, 1972, p. 110.
5. As will be seen in subsequent chapters, this belief has continued within Islamic political thought up to the present day.
6. Quoted in Hourani, *Arab Thought in the Liberal Age 1798–1939*, London, Oxford University Press, 1962, p. 77.
7. Quoted in Jad'an, p. 154.
8. Ibid.
9. Al-Afghani, 'Refutation of the Materialists', in Majed Fakhry, *A History of Islamic Philosophy*, 2nd edn, New York, Columbia University Press, 1983, p. 336.
10. Quoted in Ali al-Mahafdha, *al-Itijahat al-Fikriyah ind al-'Arab*, 2nd edn, Beirut, al-Ahliyah lil Nashr wal Tawzie', 1978, p. 77.
11. Quoted in Muhammad 'Umarah, *al-Turath fi Daw'i al-agl*, Beirut, Dar al-Wahda, 1980, p. 211.
12. 'Umarah, *al-'Amal al-Kamilati Rifa'a al-Tahtawi*, p. 16.
13. Khayr al-Din al-Tunisi, op. cit., p. 77.
14. Ibid., p. 76.
15. Alij Mubarak, *'Ilm al-Din*, 1, Alexandria, Mahrusa Press, 1882, p. 308.
16. Quoted in Jad'an, op. cit., p. 143.
17. Ibid.
18. Quoted in Hourani, op. cit., p. 79.
19. *Al-Urwa al-Wathga*, 2nd edn, Beirut, Dar al-Katib al-Arabi, 1980, p. 88.
20. Quoted in Jad'an, op. cit., p. 327.
21. Ibid., p. 328.
22. *Al-Siyasah*, Cairo, 19 June 1933.
23. Quoted in Jad'an, op. cit., p. 332.
24. Quoted in Jad'an, op. cit., p. 332.
25. Quoted in Jad'an, op. cit., p. 333.
26. Ibid.
27. Ali Abd al-Razik, *al-Islam wa 'Usul al-Hukm*, Beirut, al-Mu'asasah al-Arabiyah lil Dirasat wa al-Nashir, 1972.
28. Ibid., p. 129.
29. Ibid., p. 136.
30. Quoted in Jad'an, op. cit., p. 345.
31. Ibid.
32. Ibid., pp. 346–8.
33. Ibid., p. 348.
34. Hasan al-Banna, *Rasiel al-Imam al-Shahid*, Beirut, Mu'asasat al-Risala, n.d., pp. 388–97.
35. Ibid., p. 397.

36. Abd al-Rahman al-Bazzaz, *Min Ruh al-Islam*, Baghdad, al-Ani Press, 1959, pp. 191–2.
37. Ibid., p. 56.
38. Ibid.
39. Quoted in Jad'an, op. cit., p. '371.
40. Quoted in Jad'an, op. cit., p. 375.
41. Ibid., p. 376.
42. Ibid., pp. 376–7.
43. Ibid., p. 377.
44. Ibid.
45. Ibid.
46. Quoted in Jad'an, op. cit., p. 509.
47. Ibid.
48. Ibid.
49. Ibid., p. 510.
50. Ibid., p. 514.
51. Ibid.
52. Ibid.
53. Ibid., p. 516.
54. Sayyid [Kotb], *Social Justice in Islam*, trans. J.B. Hardie, New York, Octagon Books, 1970, p. 24.
55. Ibid., p. 27.
56. Ibid., p. 43.
57. Ibid., p. 105.
    Ibid., p. 138.
58. Khaled Muhammad Khaled, *Min Huna Nabd'a*, 10th edn, Cairo, Muasasat
59. al-Khanchi, 1963, p. 51.
    Mustafa al-Siba'i, *Ishtra Kiyat al-Islam*, Damascus, Damascus University
60. Press, 1959.
    Ibid., p. 99.
61. Ibid.
62. Ibid., p. 115.
63. Sheikh Mahmud Shaltut, 'al-Ishtiakiyya wa-al-Islam' (Socialism and
64. Islam), *al-Jumhuriyyah*, Cairo, 22 December 1961. Excerpted and translated in Kemal H. Karpat (ed.), *Political and Social Thought in the Contemporary Middle East*, rev. edn, New York, Praeger, 1982, pp. 108–15.

Part II

Modern Activism

3   The Muslim Brotherhood

The philosophy and early history of the Muslim Brotherhood (Ikhwan) were fundamentally shaped by the organization's founder the first leader, Hassan al-Banna.[1] Al-Banna was born in October 1906 in the small town of Mahmudiyya, north-west of Cairo; he was the son of the village Imam and watchmaker.[2] He attended primary school there, and later a local teacher-training school and the Dar al-Ulum in Cairo, where Arabic and related subjects were taught. Al-Banna graduated from Dar al-Ulum in the summer of 1927; in September of that year he accepted a position as a teacher of Arabic in a primary school in Ismailia.

Although only 21 years old, al-Banna had already demonstrated a profound commitment to Islam and a deeply-felt concern about the corruption of Islamic society by the materialism and secularism of the West. While at primary school, al-Banna had participated in a number of local student Islamic organizations. He had also become intensely interested in Sufism, eventually becoming a fully initiated member of a Sufi order in 1922. Al-Banna continued his involvement with Islamic organizations during his studies in Cairo. His increased contact with external, non-Islamic influences and his observation of the submissiveness and corruption of the Egyptian Islamic establishment at al-Azhar and elsewhere reinforced his view that active Islamic teaching, counselling and guidance were needed to reverse the corruption of society and religion. Ismailia – with its British military camps and Suez Canal Company offices, and its concomitant contrasts between wealthy foreigners and impoverished Egyptians – had a similar effect on the young teacher.

On arriving in Ismailia, al-Banna became an active supporter of the Young Men's Muslim Association and a correspondent for the journal it published, *Majallat al-Fath*. In 1928 al-Banna formed his own organization – The Society of Muslim Brothers (al-Ikhwan al-Muslimun). According to Abd al-Adhim Ramadhan, a student of contemporary Egyptian political history:

The formation of the Muslim Brethren movement was not motivated by political objectives connected to national issues of the constitution, and independence, or the rejection of the existing political system. Rather, it was motivated by Salafi political thought to reject the current of Westernization. The idea of violence to reach power was not an intention of the organizers. Rather, the intent was to work peacefully through the publication of newspapers, formation of associations, propagation and guidance.[3]

Initial organization activities were centred on Ismailia, and met with considerable success. Ikhwan membership rapidly expanded and, by 1930, a new headquarters was built for the organization in town. Furthermore, the Ikhwan sponsored a number of local projects in Ismailia, including a mosque, a boys' club and school, and a girls' school. Within a few years al-Banna had extended his activities to neighbouring areas, and by 1932 Ikhwan branches could be found in Port Sa'id, Suez, and several other locations, with the Ismailia branch acting as headquarters.

In 1932 al-Banna was transferred, at his own request, from Ismailia to a teaching post in Cairo, where he resumed his activities in semi-secrecy. He soon presided over a merger between his group and the Society for Islamic Culture,[4] after which the Cairo branch became the new headquarters of the rapidly expanding Ikhwan. Between 1933 and 1939, the Ikhwan held five general conferences, which formulated the basic policy positions of the organization, according to Richard P. Mitchell, author of the most definitive English-language study of the movement.[5]

The fifth conference was also the tenth anniversary of the movement. These ten years had produced a set of ideas which, though general in form, was the foundation of the ideology of the Society and the substance of its appeal for the next ten years and beyond. These ideas were, essentially, a definition of 'the Islam of the Muslim Brother'; the insistence on (1) Islam as a total system, complete unto itself, and the final arbiter of life in all its aspects; (2) an Islam formulated from and based on its two primary sources, the revelation in the Qur'ān and the wisdom of the Prophet in the Sunna; and (3) an Islam applicable to all times and to all places.

Within this framework, Banna defined for the members the scope of the movement of which they were a part: 'The idea of the Muslim Brothers included in it all categories of reform'. In specific terms he defined the movement as 'a Salafiyya message, a Sunni way, a Sufi truth, a political organization, an athletic group, a cultural-educational union, an economic company, and a social idea'.

From its first general conference in May 1933 onwards, the Ikhwan issued letters to the political leaders of Egypt (and other Islamic countries), regarding issues of concern: the first (to King Fu'ad in 1933) regarding Christian missionary activity; later ones to King Faruq and successive Egyptian prime ministers, regarding the need for Islamic spiritual and social reform. It was not until the end of the decade, however, that the organization adopted a more aggressive political stance. This was declared in May 1938, in al-Banna's editorial in the first issue of *al-Nadhir*, a new Muslim Brotherhood weekly:

We are moving from propagation alone to propagation accompanied by struggle and action. We will direct our call at the responsible leadership of the country: the notables, the government, and all the rulers, sheikhs, legislators, and political parties. We will try to call them to our goals. We will place our programmes at their disposal. If they respond to our call and adopt the path to our aim, we support them. But if they resort to evasion . . . then we are at war with every leader, every president of a party and every organization that does not work for the victory of Islam. Till now you have not confronted a political party of organization. You did not join them either . . . . Your position . . . was passive in the past. But today, in this new stage, it will not be that way. You will strongly oppose all of those whether they are in power or not . . . . If they do not respond to you by accepting the teaching of Islam as their programme for action . . . [the choice] is either loyalty or animosity . . . . It's not our fault that politics is part of religion. Islam includes both the subjects and the rulers. 'Give unto Caesar what is Caesar's; and give unto God what is God's' is not the teaching of Islam. Islam teaches that Caesar and what belongs to him are for the Almighty God, and God alone.[6]

Similarly, speaking to the fifth general conference in January 1938,[7]

. . . the time when you will have – Oh ye Muslim Brethren – three hundred phalanxes, each one of them equipped spiritually with faith and principle, mentally with science and culture, and

physically with training and exercise; at that time ask me to
plunge with you into the depths of the seas, to rend the skies with
you, and to attack every stubborn tyrant; then, God willing, I will
do it.[8]

The ideology of Hassan al-Banna

With its fifth general conference, al-Ikhwan al-Muslimun celebrated
the first ten years of its existence. During these years, and in the ten
years of his life which followed them, al-Banna provided his followers
with a coherent and explicit analysis of the ills of contemporary
society, and with an Islamic path of spiritual, social, economic and
political reforms through which such ills might be confronted and
overcome. Indeed, al-Banna's well-developed and well-explicated
ideology proved to have a substantial impact on Egypt and the Middle
East in general, its effects being felt more than thirty-five years after his
assassination in 1949.

Al-Banna saw around him an Islamic world beset by poverty,
corruption and weakness. Politically, the Islamic countries were
assailed by 'imperialist aggression on the part of their enemies, and by
factionalism, rivalry, division, and disunity on the part of their sons'.[9]
Economically, they were subject to 'the propagation of usurious
practices throughout all their social classes, and the exploitation of
their resources and natural treasures by foreign companies.'[10]
Intellectually and sociologically, they suffered from anarchy, licen-
tiousness, and a loss of faith, hope and humanity. Secularism and
imitation of the West had become commonplace. Even much of the
religious establishment had become cowardly and impotent.

To all these miserable conditions, al-Banna and the Muslim
Brotherhood offered a solution: the path of Islam. This path was not
conceived as simply being a narrow, spiritual one; rather, Islam was
seen as representing an all-encompassing system of guidance in social,
economic, and political conduct:

We believe that the principles and teachings of Islam are
comprehensive, governing the affairs of men in this world and in
the next, and those who think that these teachings deal only with
spiritual and ritualistic aspects are mistaken in this assumption,
for Islam is: doctrine, worship, homeland, nationality, religion,
spirituality and a state, spirituality and action, scripture and
sword. The Holy Qur'ān speaks of this and considers it the
essence of Islam.[11]

No other religious or philosophical system could provide all the institutions, principles, objectives and sensitivities required for a rebirth in Egypt and the other Muslim countries. The totality of Islam was therefore central to al-Banna's thought, providing the basis not only for its analyses and prescriptions, but also for its internal coherence and popular appeal.

Thus, put simply, the Muslim Brotherhood saw itself as the vanguard of Islam. According to the Ikhwan view of history, the neglect of Islam had begun in the Ummayad period when, following the rule of the first four 'rightly-guided' Khalifes, Islam was increasingly corrupted and neglected, replaced by the imperatives and decadence of dynastic rule. In turn, this failure to follow the true path of Islam weakened Islamic civilization: religious schisms and political factionalism became more acute, while a resurgent Europe extended its power. This process of Islamic decline came to a climax in the aftermath of the First World War, with colonial domination of the Middle East, the onslaught of Zionism in Palestine, and the spread of Western secularism and materialism as symbolized by Ataturk's abolition of the *Khalafah* and the adoption of Western political-legal systems in Turkey, Egypt, and elsewhere in the Islamic world.

It was in opposition to Western colonialism and imperialism that the Ikhwan directed much of its energy. In his tract, *Bayn al-Ams wa al-Yawm*, al-Banna outlined the two 'fundamental goals' of the Muslim Brethren as follows:

1. That the Islamic fatherland be freed from all foreign domination, for this is a natural right belonging to every human being which only the unjust oppressor or the conquering exploiter will deny.

2. That a free Islamic state may arise in this free fatherland, acting according to the precepts of Islam, applying its social regulations, proclaiming its sound principles, and its sage mission to all mankind. For, as long as this state does not emerge, the Muslims in their totality are committing sin, and are responsible before God the Lofty, the Great, for their failure to establish it and their slackness in creating it.[12]

These goals were to be realized within the territories of historic Islam, i.e. 'the Nile Valley and the Arab domain, and in every land which God has made fortunate through the Islamic creed'.[13] Muslim Brethren were also directed to work towards the reform of education; to struggle against poverty, ignorance, disease and crime; and to create an 'exemplary society which will deserve to be associated with the Islamic Sacred Law'.[14]

Because of Islam's status as an all-embracing system of social knowledge, al-Banna saw within it guidance on matters of strategy as well as on matters of diagnosis and cure. His descriptions of the tasks confronting the Brotherhood were thus always amply supported by Qur'ānic citations and the sayings of the Prophet. Within the organization, strong emphasis was placed on the overriding importance of deep faith, precise organization, uninterrupted work, obedience and determined leadership. Because of the multi-faceted nature of Islam, al-Banna constantly stressed that the Ikhwan was not a narrow political or religious grouping. Instead, he asserted that it was all of these and more:

1. It's a Salafi movement: it pursues the return of Islam to the purity of its source in the Qur'ān and the Tradition of the Prophet.
2. It's a Sunni order: it is modelled on the Sunna in everything, particularly in matters of belief and worship . . .
3. It's a Sufi reality: it operates on the principle that virtue is in the purity of the soul, innocence of the heart, hard work . . .
4. It's a political organization: it demands reform in internal politics, changes in the relationship between Islamic nation and the outside world, and the education of the people for integrity, self-respect and national consciousness.
5. It's an athletic club: it promotes good health . . . since the duties of Islam cannot be fulfilled without good health . . .
6. It's a scientific and cultural society: because Islam makes the search for knowledge an imperative of every Muslim and the Ikhwan in reality is a school for education, an institute [dedicated] to caring for body, mind and spirit.
7. It's an economic enterprise: because Islam deals with the acquisition and management of wealth . . .
8. It's a social idea: it deals with the problem of Islamic society and attempts to find solutions . . . .[15]

Despite its militancy and later violence, the Muslim Brotherhood generally eschewed the revolutionary path to reform. Section 2, Article 4 of the Brotherhood's 1945 basic regulations, for example, stated that 'The Brethren will always prefer gradual advancement and development, productive work, and co-operation with lovers of good and truth. They do not wish harm to anyone, no matter what his religion, race or country'.[16] Al-Banna himself reserved the use of revolutionary force to those occasions only when no other path of reform was open:

> The Brethren will use practical force whenever there is no other way and whenever they are sure the implements of faith and unity are ready. Whenever they use force they will be honourable and outspoken. They will warn first and wait a while, then they will advance in dignity and strength. They will bear all the consequences of their behaviour in satisfaction and content.[17]

Instead, the Ikhwan primarily sought to achieve its goals gradually through the recruitment of new members and the propagation of its message; through the initiation of carefully selected Islamic projects of its own; and by offering advice and guidance to the government of the day.[18] The first and second of these strategies can be seen in the Ikhwan's emphasis on organization and propaganda organs, and in its sponsorship of mosques, schools, clubs and other local projects. The latter strategy can be seen within the Ikhwan's post-1933 practice of sending letters to the King and his ministers. Examination of these letters sheds considerable light on both the reform programme, and the priorities, of the Brotherhood.

One such letter – *Nahwa al-Nur* (Toward the Light)[19] – was written by al-Banna to King Faruq, to Prime Minister Mustafa al-Nahhas Pasha, to the rulers of other Islamic countries, and to various religious and civic notables, in 1947. In it, al-Banna argued that the Islamic world had reached a crossroads at which it must choose between two competing paths of development: the Western path, and the path of Islam. Western civilization, he noted, had achieved much. But those achievements were now crumbling amid tyranny, economic crises, and exploitation due to the inherently blind and misguided nature of the Western path. Thus revealed, the way of Western civilization had little to commend it.

The way of Islam, on the other hand, promised to solve all the problems of the West. It, more than any other ideology, belief or system of social organization, provided the basis for national resurgence: 'There is no regime in this world which will supply the renascent nation with what it requires in the way of institutions, principles, objectives, and sensibilities to the same extent as does Islam to every one of its renascent nations . . . . No nation adheres to [Islam] without succeeding in its aspirations.'[20]

Islam provides hope for the weak. Islam brings national greatness through divine sanctification. It concerns itself with the strengthening of just armed forces, with the quality of public health, with the provision of a superior morality, with the fostering of a sound economy, and with the creation of appropriate public institutions. Contrary to what some may think, adherence to the Islamic path does not imply intolerance of non-Muslim religious minorities. Nor need an Islamic resurgence necessarily lead to increased friction with the West.

Of particular interest in *Nahwa al-Nur* are al-Banna's proposals for practical reforms which would characterize adherence to the Islamic path. No less than fifty such reforms are elucidated, with al-Banna offering the assistance of the Muslim Brotherhood to any government or organization which wishes to implement them.

Under the heading 'political, judicial, and administrative' reforms, al-Banna called for changes in the judicial system so as to bring it into accordance with the *Shari'a*; the infusion of Islamic principles and morality into the bureaucracy and government institutions; and the evaluation of all government action by reference to Islamic teachings. The operation of the civil service should facilitate the performance of religious duty, and the private and public behaviour of all government employees should be subject to government scrutiny. Bribery and favouritism must be ended. Party rivalry must also be ended, with all political forces within the nation channelled into a single common front. The armed forces should be strengthened. The government should pursue a pan-Islamic foreign policy by strengthening its ties with other Islamic countries, and by giving 'serious consideration to the matter of the departed Khalafah'.[21]

The second set of reforms proposed by al-Banna in *Nahwa al-Nur* was categorized as 'social and educational'. Many of these concerned public morality: al-Banna called for an end to prostitution, gambling, dancing, ostentatious dress, and Western customs; support for traditional family life and the treatment of women in accordance with Islamic principles; and the enforcement of an Islamic moral code through the censorship of speeches, books, plays, radio broadcasts and the cinema. Public health care should be expanded, and attention be given to hygiene and a clean water supply within the villages.

Education should be reformed by increasing its religious content, and by affiliating village primary schools with the mosques. Increased emphasis should be placed on the teaching of Arabic, and Islamic history. Male and female students should be segregated, with each learning a distinct and appropriate curriculum. A literacy programme should be instituted through the cafés. The entire educational system should be orientated towards raising the general level of education, bringing different cultures together, and 'inculcating a virtuous, patriotic spirit and an unwavering moral code'.[22]

Third, al-Banna proposed a number of 'economic' reforms. First, among these was the reorganization of the Zakat (alms tax), and the use of funds so raised for benevolent projects and the strengthening of the armed forces. Usury should be prohibited, and the masses protected from exploitation by monopolies. Productivity, income and employment should be increased; natural resources exploited; and foreign projects nationalized. Civil service salaries should be adjusted so as to increase the pay of junior civil servants and decrease that of senior civil servants, with the total number of government posts to be reduced.

The specific reform proposals put forward by Hasan al-Banna and the Muslim Brotherhood in Nahwa al-Nur obviously do not represent the totality of the Brotherhood's social, political and economic agenda. Elsewhere, for example, one finds al-Banna calling for land reform, labour organization, social security and the redistribution of wealth.[23] Nevertheless, Nahwa al-Nur does illustrate well the emphasis that the Muslim Brotherhood placed on the improvement of society through a fundamental 'Islamification' of people's beliefs and moral codes, as well as of formal government institutions.

No survey of the principles and programme of Hasan al-Banna and the Ikhwan al-Muslimun would be complete without a brief outline of their attitude towards other contemporary ideologies. In particular, it is important to examine al-Banna's view of communism, fascism and Western liberal democracy; his relationship with nationalism and national patriotism; and his position regarding non-Muslim religions and the various schisms and trends within Islam itself.

Al-Banna perceived a number of positive features within the Western ideologies of fascism, communism and liberal democracy. Fascism inspired 'martial strength and military preparedness'; communist doctrine displayed concern for the poor, for equality, and for social justice; the liberal democracies stood for individual liberties and representative government. These positive features were, however, more than outweighed by the dysfunctions of each system. The communist nations suffered from tyranny and domestic oppression. The Western democracies were prone to a surfeit of individualism, moral decay and capitalist economic exploitation. Both communism and capitalism were based on the inherently corrupting concepts of materialism and secularism.[24]

With regard to the question of nationalism and national patriotism, the Ikhwan strongly supported nationalist issues. The struggle against Western political, economic and cultural domination over the Islamic world was (as has already been shown) one of the Muslim Brotherhood's two 'fundamental goals' Their reform proposals reflected a concern for strong national defence, for nationalization of foreign enterprises, and the elimination of Western socio-cultural influences. Moreover, many Brethren did (as will be seen later) actively risk their lives in the fight against Zionism in Palestine and against the British in the Canal Zone.

Nonetheless, the Ikhwan's ideological relationship with nationalism is more complex than appearances first suggest, essentially revolving around their anti-imperialism and their pan-Islamic aspirations.[25] Al-Banna did argue that distinct nations existed, each with its 'own distinct qualities and particular moral characteristics', with the Arab nations enjoying the 'fullest and most abundant share' of such qualities.[26] He also lauded patriotism, in that it implied attachment to the land, love of freedom, and commitment to the community. He condemned, however, all conceptions of patriotism which implied factionalism, and all conceptions of nationalism which were based on 'aggression', 'victimization' and 'racial self-aggrandizement'.[27] Instead of the patriotism of territorial boundaries and the nationalism of racism, the Muslim Brotherhood was said to stand for patriotism to the Islamic community, and a nationalism based on the glorification of past piety and bravery, with the nation standing as a focus of individual strivings.[28] To al-Banna and the Ikhwan, 'The bonds of credal doctrine . . . [are] . . . holier than those of blood or soil'.[29]

With regard to the treatment of non-Muslim religious minorities, the Brotherhood's stated policy was one of tolerance. This principle was echoed in the organization's 1945 basic regulations, as well as in al-Banna's writings. The Brotherhood was, however, vehemently opposed to what it saw as imperialism in religious garb: Christian and Jewish 'Crusaderism', exemplified by Christian missionary activity and the Zionist colonization of Palestine, respectively. At times, this identification between Western Christianity and Western imperialism led the Muslim Brotherhood to support the Eastern (Orthodox and Coptic) Christian heritage against Western (Catholic and especially Protestant) Christian 'subversion'.[30]

As with any Islamic movement, the various divisions within the faith were of great concern to the Muslim Brotherhood. Throughout his writings, al-Banna was careful to stress that the Ikhwan's Islamic message was a general one, and that the Muslim Brotherhood was 'unaffiliated with any particular sect' within Islam.[31] He argued that disagreement within religion was unavoidable, and perhaps even useful in so far as it lent flexibility to faith and allowed it to endure. It was important, however, that such differences did not divide the *umma*, and prevent the Muslim community from achieving its goal.

The second decade: 1939–1949

As noted above, the late 1930s saw the fully-fledged entrance of the Muslim Brotherhood onto the political stage, in Egypt and in other Islamic countries. It was, more than any other issue, circumstances in Palestine which facilitated this entrance and geographic expansion. When the Palestinian Arab revolt against British colonial rule and Zionist immigration broke out in 1936, the Ikhwan seized upon the occasion to carry out active anti-British propaganda throughout Egypt. During the three years of the revolt (1936–39), the Ikhwan came into contact with the Mufti of Jerusalem, and raised funds for the Palestinian cause. They also came into close contact with a number of Egyptian political leaders, notably (Prime Minister) 'Ali Maher and 'Abd al-Rahman Azzam, both of whom were trying to formulate an Egyptian pan-Arab policy.[32]

The Palestine issue further stimulated the growth of the Ikhwan: the total number of Ikhwan branches grew from roughly 15 in 1932 to 300 in 1938, to 500 in 1940.[33] These included, after 1937, a branch in Syria, based in Aleppo and covering Syria and Lebanon; and agents in a number of other Arab countries.[34] Ikhwan membership was drawn from most social classes, and was predominantly rural or urban working-class in composition. Despite this, the leadership and the most active cadres of the Ikhwan were dominated by Egyptians from urban middle-class backgrounds.[35]

The Muslim Brotherhood's very success soon sparked off challenges to it, and ushered in a period of tribulation for the movement. This was not unforeseen, for even as the Brotherhood had embarked on the path of active politics, al-Banna had warned his followers of the challenges ahead:

I would like to avow to you frankly that your mission is still unknown to many people, and that on the day they find out about it and grasp its import and its aims, you will encounter violent antagonism and sharp hostility. You will find many hardships ahead of you, and many obstacles will rise up before you. . . . you will find among the clerical classes and the religious establishment those who will regard your understanding of Islam as outlandish, and censure your campaign on that account. Chiefs, leaders, and men of rank and authority will hate you, all governments will rise as one against you, and every government will try to set limits to your activities and to put impediments in your way. . . . Without a doubt, you will then experience trials and tribulations, you will be imprisoned, arrested, transported, and persecuted, and your goods will be confiscated, your employments suspended, and your homes searched.[36]

With the approach and outbreak of the Second World War, the Ikhwan continued its anti-British, pan-Islamic propaganda, officially calling for Egyptian non-belligerency in the conflict and the limitation of assistance to Britain to the minimum stipulated in the 1936 Anglo-Egyptian Treaty (i.e. a British garrison in the Canal Zone, a naval base at Alexandria, and wartime use of Egyptian communication facilities). Furthermore, al-Banna was secretly in contact with anti-British elements within the Egyptian armed forces, notably (former) Egyptian Commander-in-Chief 'Aziz al-Misri, and a junior army officer named Anwar al-Sadat. This stance led to increasing British pressure on successive Egyptian governments to deal with the Ikhwan and other anti-British movements. Eventually, in October 1941, the government of Prime Minister Sirri Pasha moved against the Muslim Brotherhood, arresting al-Banna and a few other prominent Brethren, and suppressing the weekly Ikhwan magazines *al-Ta'aruf* and *al-Shua'* and the monthly *al-Manar*. Meetings of, and press references to, the Ikhwan were also banned.[37]

Al-Banna and his colleagues were released in less than a month, due to palace intervention on the Ikhwan's behalf.[38] However, it was not until February 1942 that the Ikhwan were allowed to resume some of their activities. This, together with the imposition of government restrictions on the sale of alcohol and a clampdown on prostitution, were carried out by the new Wafdist government of Prime Minister al-Nahhas Pasha in order to placate the Ikhwan and forestall their participation in the forthcoming Egyptian elections. Thereafter, relations between the Ikhwan and Nahhas' government varied between cordiality and hostility.[39]

The dismissal of al-Nahhas and the formation of a new government under Ahmed Mahir Pasha in October 1944 saw the reimposition of many restrictions on the Brotherhood. Mahir favoured Egypt declaring war on Germany and Italy – a move that the Ikhwan vehemently opposed – and when he was assassinated in February while reading that particular declaration in the Chamber of Deputies, the Ikhwan was briefly suspected of the deed. Restrictions on the movement continued after the war under the first government of Mahir's successor, Mahmud Fahmi al-Nuqrashi Pasha.

Post-war Egypt was a country racked by political turmoil, the after-effect of a war which had seen major social changes and the rise of indigenous (pan-Arab, pan-Islamic) and imported (communist, liberal-democratic) ideologies, while simultaneously circumscribing meaningful political expression and activity. The Ikhwan found itself in competition with the Wafd for the leadership of the nationalist movement in Egypt, and in this challenge to the Wafd it found some encouragement from King Faruq, and from Prime Minister Isma'il Sidqi Pasha in 1946. The Sidqi government (February–December 1946) permitted the Ikhwan to publish its newspaper, to purchase newsprint at the official rate, and extended training and uniform privileges to the Ikhwan scout corps (Firaq al-Rihalal). Such encouragement did not, however, lead to any diminution of Ikhwan criticism of government policy. Al-Banna and his movement were constantly critical of Egyptian–British dealings regarding British withdrawal from Cairo, Alexandria and the Canal Zone, and future Anglo–Egyptian defence arrangements: 'The government of Sidqi Pasha, in its insistence on negotiations, does not represent the will of the nation; any treaty or alliance concluded by it with Britain, before the evacuation of her forces, is void and does not bind the nation.'[40]

The Brotherhood played a prominent role in the student and industrial unrest which accompanied the negotiations. It also engaged in periodic violence against British military targets in Egypt, and occasionally against the Egyptian government itself. These latter actions were carried out by the Muslim Brotherhood's 'secret apparatus', a covert paramilitary unit of up to one thousand members (1948), probably formed in the early 1940s. According to the only scholarly study of this paramilitary unit:

All evidence points out during this period [that] al-Banna was working to transform the Ikhwan from a civilian group into a para-military organization and move from the stage of peaceful propagation through love, brotherhood and friendship to the stage of readiness to implement its aims by force. Al-Banna began building a huge army under the innocent name of Firaq al-Rihalal.[41]

The rapid growth of militant anti-British sentiment was complemented by a growing crisis in Palestine. As during the 1936–39 Palestine revolt, the Muslim Brotherhood was vociferous in its support for the Palestinian Arab cause. Arms were acquired; paramilitary training missions despatched to Palestine; and Brethren were trained and mobilized for future military service in the country, with the first Ikhwan 'battalion' ready for action by October 1947. Several weeks before the 'official' outbreak of the Palestine war and the formal intervention of Egyptian and other Arab armies on 15 May 1948, Muslim Brotherhood irregulars began infiltrating into Palestine and fighting alongside Palestinian forces. Eventually, some 400 or so Brethren were to see action in Palestine in this way.[42]

The years 1945–48 were ones of considerable expansion for the Muslim Brotherhood. Their anti-British activities and their clear commitment to the Palestinian cause, as well as their social ideology, were well received by the Egyptian masses. Furthermore, they managed to avoid the stigmas attached to their major political competitors. Unlike the Wafd, the Ikhwan were not tainted by wartime co-operation with the British, corruption, and identification with vested interests. In contrast to the communists and their alien doctrines of proletarian struggle, the Ikhwan's Islam was understandable and attractive to the traditional population. As a result of these and other factors, the Brotherhood's support reached new heights during this period, with some estimates putting the figure at 300–600,000 members (and as many sympathizers), organized into some two thousand branches.[43] Formal or informal Muslim Brotherhood branches existed outside Egypt in Syria, Lebanon, Palestine, Transjordan, Iraq, Sudan, Eritrea, Morocco, Tunisia and other Islamic countries inside and outside the Middle East.[44]

The failure of Arab military intervention to crush the nascent state of Israel and prevent the partition of Palestine intensified civil unrest in Egypt in the second half of 1948. In this context, the Muslim Brotherhood's political success – coupled with their militancy and increasing use of violent measures – ultimately led Egyptian governments to take harsh action against the Brotherhood. Thus, on 8 December 1948, citing the Muslim Brotherhood's involvement in acts of violence and conspiracy, the al-Nuquashi government issued a military order calling for 'Disbanding of the Muslim Brethren and their branches wherever they may be, the closing of their centres, and the seizure of their papers, documents, magazine, publications, monies and properties, and all other assets of the Association'.[45] Thereafter, and despite al-Banna's best efforts, relations between the Ikhwan and the government deteriorated still further. On 28 December 1948, a member of the Muslim Brotherhood's 'secret apparatus' shot and killed Prime Minister al-Nuquashi as he entered the Ministry of the Interior. As a result, al-Nuquashi's successor, Prime Minister Ibrahim 'Abd al-Hadi Pasha, instituted a ruthless campaign of arrests and property seizure against the outlawed organization.

Al-Banna deeply regretted the assassination and the government reaction to it. He had second thoughts as to the wisdom of the Ikhwan's entrance into formal politics, and wrote that future Muslim Brotherhood activities might best be confined to education and advocation within the framework of existing political parties:

The thought which I have conceived is that our organization should take upon itself the raising of the standards of the country, religiously, socially and economically – neglecting the political aspects – and to permit outstanding members of the association to present themselves for the elections under the auspices of whatever parties they see fit to join; provided that they do not join any one party and provided they undertake the spreading of the mission of the association within these parties .... I believe the time is not far distant when these parties will have faith in what we advocate.[46]

It was, however, too late. On 12 February 1949 Hasan al-Banna – founder, Director-General, and guiding force of al-Ikhwan al-Muslimun – was assassinated outside the headquarters of the Young Men's Muslim Association by members of the Egyptian secret police.[47]

The Muslim Brotherhood after al-Banna

Al-Banna's death was a severe blow to the Muslim Brotherhood, as were the seven months of continued suppression under the al-Hadi government which followed it. Eventually, however, the Society's oppression was lessened with the accession to power of a Wafdist government under Nahas. Gradually the organization got arrested members released, regained its property, started publication of its newspapers, and became openly active in politics once more. Hasan Ismail al-Hudaybi, a former judge, was elected the new Director-General of the movement. His open condemnation of past Ikhwan violence, his dislike of the 'secret apparatus', and his apparent accommodation with the palace, stimulated initial opposition to his leadership, which presaged the internecine feuding that would plague the society throughout the 1950s.

Despite involvement in guerrilla warfare against the British in the Canal Zone, the Brotherhood maintained a relatively low political profile until the July 1952 Egyptian revolution. Prior to the revolution, the Muslim Brotherhood had contact with the Free Officers' movement. In fact, several prominent members of the Free Officers movement maintain that the Muslim Brotherhood leadership had prior knowledge of the date of the revolution and played a role in it by providing guards for important public buildings and mosques.[48] According to one of the original Free Officers, Ahmed Hamroosh, 'the relationship between the Free Officers and the Muslim Brotherhood was close. A number of the officers had belonged to the Ikhwan at some stage in their life . . . . When the revolution succeeded, the Ikhwan considered it their success.'[49] The 'Committee of Free Officers' undertook two measures favourable to the Ikhwan immediately following the revolution. The first was to reopen the inquiry into the assassination of Hasan al-Banna. The second was to declare a general amnesty for political prisoners, most of whom were from the Ikhwan. Moreover, in late September 1952, the Ikhwan were invited to join the Revolutionary Cabinet formed by Muhammad Najib. They responded by nominating three persons of whom only one –Sheikh Hasan al-Baquri – was accepted by the Revolutionary Command Council. He was subsequently expelled from the Muslim Brotherhood – an early sign of the tensions yet to come.

On 12 January 1953, a fifty-member constituent assembly was created to draft a new constitution, an assembly in which three Brethren sat. Al-Hudaybi and the Muslim Brotherhood called for a plebiscite to determine whether the population preferred a Western or an Islamic juridical system. 'Should they vote for Muslim law, then the constituent assembly must comply; should they vote for Western law, an impossible notion for a Muslim, we will then know ourselves and will teach the nation the bidding of the Lord and what it must do'.[50]

In early 1953 all political parties were dissolved and their activities banned. The Ikhwan, however, were exempted from the ban. Hamroosh reported that Nasser told the Minister of the Interior, Sulaiman Hafidh, that 'the Ikhwan was one of the greatest supporters of the movement . . . contributed greatly to it, and still offers continuous support.'[51] In view of this, he asked the Minister to find a way to exempt the Ikhwan from the ban on political parties and activities.[52] However, the distinction between religious associations and political parties – the distinction which allowed the Ikhwan to continue functioning freely under Law No. 179 of 1952 – was one that the Ikhwan itself ultimately rejected, bringing it to loggerheads with the government. The reason, of course, was that the Ikhwan's religious activities were political by nature. This was exemplified by their effort to have all laws scrutinized before being issued, to ensure their conformity with the *Shari'a*. To one such demand an irritated Nasser retorted in an official communiqué: 'I have already told the Guide [al-Hudaybi] that we will not accept guardianship . . . . I repeat the same today with determination and insistence'.[53]

Late in 1953 the government created a political body, the Liberation Movement, its declared aim being the formation of a united political organization to encompass all political groups, including the Ikhwan. The Brotherhood strongly rejected this step, and al-Hudaybi rushed to Nasser to inform him that

> This is not in [the Ikhwan's] interest. They are the symbols of the whole nation and must not be the symbol of a party. Furthermore, ideological parties cannot be created by army men and policemen. What will happen is that the opportunists will exploit the new organization and consequently hurt the reputation of the government and revolution.[54]

No agreement was reached on this issue, and the rift between the Ikhwan and the revolutionary government started to widen. According to Abd al-Adhim Ramadhan, there were four interrelated reasons for the rift. First, the Muslim Brotherhood was negotiating with the British on the evacuation from the Canal Zone. While these negotiations were not official, they were not clandestine either. They seem to have had the tacit approval of the Revolutionary Command Council. The rift developed when the positions of the government and the Ikhwan on British evacuation came into conflict.

Second, the Ikhwan was proselytizing for membership in the army and the police, in effect creating a potential fifth column in the armed forces. Third, the well-armed paramilitary force of the Ikhwan continued to function, posing a serious challenge to the new regime. Finally, all of the above were brought to the fore when the Ikhwan initiated contact with General Muhammad Najib to form an alliance against Abd al-Nasir.[55] As a result, in January 1954 the Revolutionary Command Council declared the Ikhwan to be a political party and ordered its disbandment. Al-Hudaybi and 449 other Brethren were arrested.

In exchange for an agreement to modify political activity, the government released the members of Ikhwan from jail and withdrew the ban on the organization. However, the Ikhwan's 'secret apparatus' escalated anti-government activity, especially in the wake of the Anglo–Egyptian accord on the evacuation of British troops from the Canal Zone. Attempts were made to organize anti-government demonstrations, and on 26 October 1954 a 'secret apparatus' operative named Mahmud 'Abd al-Latif unsuccessfully attempted to assassinate Nasser. The government hit back ruthlessly. Muslim Brotherhood property was ransacked or seized, and thousands of Brethren were arrested. In December al-Hudaybi was sentenced to life imprisonment. Mahmud 'Abd al-Latif and five others closely connected with the plot to kill Nasser were hanged.

The Ikhwan's experience with the revolutionary regime between 1952 and 1954 thus paralleled the process which had taken place during the 1940s and which had culminated in the suppression of the movement in 1948. The Ikhwan had, once again, become increasingly involved in overt opposition politics, thereby inviting government counter-measures and organizational suppression. This process of Muslim Brotherhood politicization and confrontation would occur twice more over the next thirty years, first in the mid-1960s (in opposition to Nasser), and then in the late 1970s and early 1980s (amid the turmoil before and after the assassination of Anwar al-Sadat). It derives from the nature of Ikhwan ideology, which was fundamentally threatening to both the pre- and post-revolutionary governments of Egypt.

To begin with, the Muslim Brotherhood's goals of restructuring the social, political-legal, and economic order of society in accordance with their idealization of a former ethical state – the Salafiyah state –are inherently reactionary. The social, political-legal and economic changes advocated are essentially pragmatic adoptions from attractive modern social doctrines for solutions to contemporary social problems. Thus, on socio-economic and socio-political issues, the Muslim Brotherhood is ideologically pragmatic, focusing on the issues and solutions that have popular appeal. But these are only means to an end; hence, the characteristics of pragmatism and opportunism on contemporary issues – for example, in the Ikhwan's dealings with the British and the government of Nahas; or with the British and the government of Nasser later. The end – the goal – is the re-establishment of the *Shari'a* as the law of the land. The features of ideological reaction in terms of basic organizational goals and objectives and ideological pragmatism on all other issues results ultimately in opposition to any government that does not modify legal practices in accordance with the *Shari'a*, and alliance with any group that may further this end.

Another important dimension of Muslim Brotherhood ideology is its inherent theocratic authoritarianism. This basically derives from the fact that the moral order pursued by the Brotherhood is perceived as being dictated by God and imposed by government. In effect, the function of the state is to maintain a mystified moral order. By its nature, then, government must oppose any tendency towards an increase in moral choice or moral pluralism. The doctrine is mystical, repressive, dictatorial and intolerant – thus exhibiting characteristics which were, in a European context, labelled fascist.

Notes

1. This section is based on the following sources:
    Richard P. Mitchell, *The Society of the Muslim Brothers*, London, Oxford University Press, 1969.
    Muhammad-Hasan Ahmed, *Al-Ikhwan al-Muslimun fi al-Mizan*, Egypt, al-Ikla Press, 1946;
    Ishak Musa al-Husaini, *The Moslem Brethren*, Lebanon, Khayat's College Book Cooperative, 1956.
    Hassan al-Banna, *Muthkarat al-Da'wa wa al-Da'iyah*, 2nd edn, Cairo, Dar al-Shahab, 1966.
    Rifa't al-Sa'id, *Hassan al-Banna: Mata . . . Kayf . . . wa Limatha*, Cairo, Madbouli, 1977.
    Abd al-Adhim Ramadhan, *Dirasat fi Tarikh Misr al-Mouasir*, Cairo, al-Markiz al-Arabi lil Bath wa al-Nashir, 1980.
    Tariq al-Beshry, *al-Haraka al-Siyasiyah fi Misr*, Cairo, al-Haia al-Misriyah al-Ama lil Kitab, 1972.
    J. Heyworth-Dunne, *Religious and Political Trends in Egypt*, Washington, 1950.

78   *Modern Activism*

2. Mitchell, op. cit., p. 1.
3. Abd al-Adhim Ramadhan, *Al-Ikhwan al-Muslimun wa al-Tandham al-Siri*, p. 27.
4. This latter organization was led by a younger brother of Hassan al-Banna, Abd al-Rahman al-Banna.
5. Mitchell, op. cit., p. 14.
6. Quoted in Ramadhan, op. cit., pp. 30–1.
7. The sources differ on the date of this conference: Husaini reports that it occurred in 1938 (*The Moslem Brethren*, p. 17), while Mitchell places it in January 1939 (*The Society of the Muslim Brothers*, p. 14).
8. Husaini, op. cit., p. 17.
9. Al-Banna, 'Our Mission' in *Five Tracts of Hassan al-Banna*, trans. Charles Wendell, Berkeley, University of California Press, 1978, pp. 61-2.
10. Ibid.
11. Hassan al-Banna, *Rasai'l al-Imam al-Shahid Hassan al-Banna*, Beirut, Muasasat al-Risalah, n.d., p. 269.
12. Hassan al-Banna, 'Between Yesterday and Today' in *Five Tracts of Hassan al-Banna*, pp. 31–2.
13. Al-Banna, op. cit., p. 33.
14. Ibid., p. 33.
15. Al-Banna, *Rasai'l al-Imam al-Shahid Hassan al-Banna*, pp. 273–5.
16. Quoted in Husaini, op. cit., p. 18.
17. Quoted in Husaini, op. cit., p. 104.
18. Mitchell, op. cit., p. 261.
19. Hassan al-Banna, 'Toward the Light', pp. 103–32.
20. Ibid., pp. 107–8.
21. Ibid., p. 126.
22. Ibid., pp. 127–9.
23. Mitchell, op. cit., pp. 272–93; and al-Banna, *Rasai'l al-Imam al-Shahid Hassan al-Banna*, pp. 247–343.
24. Mitchell, op. cit., pp. 224–31.
25. Some parallels can be drawn here between the Ikhwan al-Muslimun and the Arab communists. In both cases, attitudes to nationalism were defined by anti-imperialism, and by reference to the 'greater cause' of pan-Islam and proletarian internationalism respectively. The major difference between the two was that while the communists (up until the late 1960s) allowed other ideological elements to restrict any nationalist activity, the Ikhwan found nationalism and Islamic reform practically compatible, and structured their policies accordingly. The net result was the greater appeal of the Brotherhood to the ardently nationalist Arab masses in the 1950s.
26. Al-Banna, 'Our Mission', p. 55.
27. Ibid., pp. 48–54.
28. In support of this view of nationalism, al-Banna quoted from the Prophet: 'God has removed from you the arrogance of paganism and the vaunting of your ancestry: mankind springs from Adam, and Adam springs from dust. The Arab has no superiority over the non-Arab except by virtue of his piety'. Al-Banna, op. cit., p. 54.
29. Ibid., p. 55.

30. Mitchell, op. cit., pp. 229–31.
31. Al-Banna, 'Our Mission', p. 56.
32. Heyworth-Dunne, op. cit., pp. 23–8.
33. Mitchell, op. cit., p. 328.
34. Heyworth-Dunne, op. cit., p. 17.
    Husaini, op. cit., pp. 75–6.
35. Mitchell, op. cit., pp. 328–30.
36. Al-Banna, 'Between Yesterday and Today', pp. 34–5.
37. Mitchell, op. cit., pp. 22–6.
38. Ramadhan, op. cit., p. 46.
39. Ibid.
40. Quoted in Mitchell, op. cit., p. 49.
41. Ramadhan, op. cit., p. 37.
42. Walid Khalidi, *From Haven to Conquest: Readings in Zionism and the Palestine Problem Until 1948*, Beirut, Institute for Palestine Studies, 1971, pp. 867–71.
43. Heyworth-Dunne, op. cit., p. 68.
    Mitchell, op. cit., p. 328.
44. Husaini, op. cit., pp. 73–86.
45. Military Order No. 63 (8 December 1948), cited in Husaini, op. cit., p. 21.
46. *Al-Jumhur al-Misri*, Cairo, 5 February 1951, quoted in Husaini, *The Moslem Brethren*, p. 21.
47. An investigation into the assassination was carried out by the Revolutionary government in 1953–4; it found evidence of support for the deed from the Prime Minister and probably the palace. Four men were given jail sentences for their part in the crime.
48. See Ahmed Hamroosh, *Qisat Thuwrat 23 Yolyo*, 1, 2nd edn, Beirut, al-Mu'asasah al-Arabiyah lil Dirasat was al-Nashir, 1977, p. 299; Fathi Radwan, *Asrar Hikomat Yolyo*, Cairo, Madboli, n.d., pp. 145–149; Abd al-Adhim Ramadhan, *Abd al-Nasir wa Azmat Mars 1954*, Cairo, Rose al-Yusuf, 1977, pp. 107–10.
49. Hamroosh, op. cit., pp. 299–300.
50. Husaini, op. cit., p. 131.
51. Hamroosh, op. cit., p. 302.
52. Ibid.
53. *Al-Ahran*, Cairo, 15 January 1954.
54. Husaini, op. cit., p. 132.
55. Abd al-Adhim Ramadhan, *Abd al-Nasir wa Azmat Mars 1954*, pp. 127–45.

4 Contemporary Islamic Political Activism: Iran

As discussed in Chapter 1, Shiism is a religious doctrine which started out as a political protest movement regarding the question of succession after the death of the Prophet Muhammad. However, this conflict did not crystallize into a clearly defined religious and political ideology until after the death of Uthman Ibn Affan, the fourth Khalife, and the ensuing controversy between the party of Ali Ibn Abi Taleb and the Ummayad dynasty. Thus, Shiism developed as a movement protesting the political legitimacy of established authority. This evolved into the central belief of Shiah doctrine, that the Imam is the legitimate ruler, and that any other government is therefore an usurpation of one of the Imam's rights. The Imam is the executive authority of God on earth. God is the ultimate ruler and Muhammad was the best and last of God's representatives to rule the Islamic community. The Imam is a 'universal authority' in religious and temporal affairs who is infallible. He commands what God ordained and prohibits what is disapproved by God. Belief in the disappearance of the true Imam and his ultimate return to establish perfect government is the foundation of Shiah theology. During the occultation of the Imam (*ghaybah*), the principal duty of the Shiite is to prepare for his return.

The Ithna'ashri (or Imamiyah) school, the dominant Shiah school in Iran, believe that there were a chain of twelve Imams directly descended from Muhammad; and that the twelfth Imam, Muhammad al-Muntezar, disappeared in 265h. (AD 878). After the occultation of the last Imam, the process of rational interpretation of the Qur'ān and Hadith (*ijtihad*), and the recognition of 'Marja'-i Taqlid' (a learned *ulama* capable of providing authoritative interpretations) became important. These institutions provided the basis whereby one or more of the most distinguished religious authorities provided leadership for the people in religious and temporal affairs.[1]

The doctrine of the occultation of the last Imam and his reappearance, to rule in a just and egalitarian manner in accordance with the precepts of the Qur'ān and Islamic law, dominated Shiah religious and political thought. Therefore, a government other than that of the Imam is unjust, a position which was reinforced in Shiah doctrine by the persistent harassment and suppression which the Shiites had to endure throughout a significant period of Islamic history. In the face of this oppression and the expectation of the Imam's return, Shiah theory developed the doctrine of '*taqiyah*', a dissimulation of religious and political beliefs. This has been used to justify an apparent acceptance of existing governments. The imposition of Shiism as a national religion in Persia by the Safavids in the sixteenth century, and the decline of centralized state power in the post-Safavid period, also served to stimulate the politicization of Shiism. In the former case, this was manifest in the creation of a structured religious hierarchy to deal with the exigencies of administering a state religion. In the latter case, the effective devolution of power to the local level which accompanied the weakening of central governments in Persia led the local clergy to assume a greater political-legal administrative role.[2]

This political role became increasingly important in Iranian politics in the late nineteenth century. Foreign domination (British and Russian at the time), as well as the existence of a tyrannical rule in Iran, the Qajar dynasty, gave a great impetus to the role of the Shiah clergy in Iranian politics. The rise of constitutional democracies encouraged secularist writers, such as Akhund Zadah, Majd al-Mulk, Mirza Sipahasalar A'zam, Mustashar al-Dawlah and others to pave the way for the dissemination of constitutional ideas among the intelligentsia in Iran. Because such ideas, as propagated by the secularist intellectuals, did not have mass support among the Iranian people, the intellectuals sought to align themselves with the clergy who seemed to command popular support. An important figure in bringing about this alliance and in bridging the gap between the two forces was Jamal al-Din Afghani. However, the interplay between the Shiah concept of true government, and the clergy's view of the contemporary political order as being unjust, dictatorial, a tool of foreign powers and therefore un-Islamic, was, perhaps, an even more significant factor in bringing about this alliance.

The support of the clergy for the constitutionalist forces in Iran during the late nineteenth and early twentieth centuries can be understood in terms of the fundamental religious significance that Shiism assigns to issues of political power and authority. The clergy supported the constitutional struggle as a means of getting rid of tyranny and foreign influence:

To protect religion, to revive the Islamic homeland, and to improve the condition of the country. We aimed at the progress of the people and the enforcing of religious laws; we wanted to put an end to embezzlement and to improve financially the army and other state affairs; we attempted to terminate aggression and imposition of a few selfish and stubborn persons.[3]

Under these circumstances, the contradiction posed, on the one hand, by the usurpation of the Imam's right, and on the other, by the necessity of government during his absence, forced Shiah intellectuals to deal theoretically with the structure and functions of power in the less than ideal state. Concepts of constitutionalism and democracy were incorporated into the Shiah theory of government to deal with the problems of the nature and origins of power during the Imam's absence, the limitations of the usurpation of power, accountability, etc., in the less than ideal state.

Sheikh Ismail Mahallati, a prominent *ulama* leader in the constitutional struggle, identified three types of government: first, rule of the infallible Imam; second, an absolute tyrannical monarchy; third, limited and constitutional form of government: 'If the Ulama do not participate in the constitutional movement, the politics of the Islamic country will follow the European model. Therefore it is compulsory for them to lend a hand to the politicians to establish laws which are in accordance with Islam.'[4]

One of the most outstanding and influential religious leaders in the struggle for constitutionalism in Iran at the beginning of this century was Mirza Muhammad Husayn Na'ini. The significance of Na'ini lies in the fact that he tried to reconcile the ideas of constitutionalism (*mashruta*) and the principles of Islamic government. He put forward two general principles for a government: first, maintaining internal order, protection of the individual's rights, education, etc. Second, 'preventing any foreign intervention . . ., preparing a defensive force and war ammunitions, and the like'.[5] There are two kinds of government: '*Tamallukiyyah*' or tyranny; and '*Vilayatiyyah*' or constitutional government. Na'ini argued that tyrannical rule turns human beings into slaves; therefore it is a duty of every Muslim to fight it.[6] In a constitutional government: 'Rulership here is based on the performance of certain duties in the interests of the public. The ruler's authority is limited to those duties, and he has no right to transgress this limit . . . . Everyone has the right to protest and is not to be subjugated or subdued by the ruler.'[7]

Na'ini held to the Shiah doctrine that the ideal government is the government of the Imam who is infallible, immune from sin, and 'possesses God-given knowledge'. However, in the absence of an Imam, 'the only possibility left . . . is to choose a constitutional form of government, even though the latter would still be a usurpation of the Imam's authority'.[8] To remove oppression of the Imam, as a result of a ruler assuming power which rightly belongs to the Imam, Na'ini argued that this can be done by the ruler's gaining the *ulama's* approval.[9] Hence his support for Article 2 of the Supplementary Fundamental Law which was added to the Persian Constitution on 7 October 1906. This article stated:

At no time must any legal enactment of the National Consultative Assembly . . . be at variance with the sacred principles of Islam . . . . It is hereby declared that it is for the . . . ulama . . . to determine whether such laws as may be proposed are or are not conformable to the principles of Islam; and it is therefore officially enacted that there shall at all times exist a committee of not less than five mujtahids . . . so that they may . . . reject and repudiate, wholly or in part, any such proposal which is at variance with the Sacred Law of Islam, so that it shall not obtain the title of legality.[10]

This article gave the clergy, for the first time, an official role in determining the compatibility of laws with Islam as well as their right to abrogate laws that are inconsistent with Islamic principles. However, the article, like the constitution itself, remained an illusion, for the Shah effectively counteracted its limitations upon his powers. Nevertheless, the constitution symbolized the population's desire for responsible government under the guidance of religious principles.

The political role of the Iranian clergy declined in the aftermath of the 1905–6 Constitutional revolution. During the reign of the first Pahlavi Shah, Reza Khan (1921–41), the clergy proved unable to offer sustained and co-ordinated opposition to reforms which weakened, and finally eliminated, the powers of religious courts; usurped the administration of *waqfs* (Islamic endowments); and encroached upon the traditional areas of clerical influence.[11] Nor was there significant clerical opposition to the first thirteen years of rule by Reza Khan's son and successor, Muhammad Reza Pahlavi. Political inactivity on the part of the Iranian clergy ended, however, with the 1953 CIA-engineered coup which deposed the nationalist government of Prime

Minister Muhammad Mossadeq and reinstalled the Shah. Thereafter, the Shiah clergy became a focus for anti-Pahlavi sentiment.[12]

Although the Iranian clergy lost the initiative following the 1905–6 Constitutional revolution, the synthesis of constitutionalism and Shiah philosophy brought to the fore in Shiah political theory the problem of the nature of government in the less than ideal state. One of the outstanding theorists who facilitated the transition of Iranian intellectuals and students to a commitment to a new revolutionary concept of Islam and to the Islamic revolutionary movement was Ali Shari'ati. Considered the 'precursor' and the 'martyred teacher' of the 1979 Iranian revolution, Shari'ati's writings and ideas became one of the main sources for political awareness programmes on the radio during the revolution in Iran.

Ali Shari'ati

Born in 1932, Shari'ati was the son of a religious authority and intellectual (*ulama*). Reflecting the nature of the milieu in which he grew up, in the late forties, he and his father joined a small circle of intellectuals, Nahzat-i Khoda Parastan-i Sosivalist (Theological Society) that was attempting to reconcile European socialist ideas with Shiite theology. The kind of moral-intellectual bent suggested by such activities was a legacy Shari'ati inherited from his father. In 1959 he went to France to study for a doctorate in sociology at the Sorbonne. In the volatile Paris setting of student activism in the early sixties, Shari'ati became involved in student organizations supporting Third World liberation movements. He translated into Persian a number of revolutionary treatises on Third World liberation.

Shari'ati returned to Iran in 1964 where, after a brief period of arrest following his arrival, he began teaching at Mashhad University. He was expelled from his post in 1968, due to his political teachings. He continued his lectures on Islam and resumed teaching at the privately-supported North Tehran Irshad Husayniyah School. The school was later closed by the Shah and Shari'ati was jailed for two years. In 1977 he was finally allowed to leave Iran for London. He died a month later, the victim either of a heart attack (according to the British) or of assassination by the Shah's secret police, SAVAK (according to his followers).

The religious, social and political doctrine put forward by Shari'ati is powerful and multi-faceted. Nevertheless, it is possible to identify within it certain core features.[13]

1. Islam is a dynamic and flexible religion that can be adapted to the modern world and to the conditions of modern-day societies. Islam, he urged the students and intellectuals, should be looked upon as an advanced revolutionary theory that combines social science with history and politics.
2. In contrast, Western liberal democratic and Marxist ideology have failed to liberate humanity from oppression. Instead, they have degenerated into materialism, thereby reducing man to an apathetic economic animal, driven by egoism and exploited by others (capitalism); or to a pawn of historical development and a slave to the state, whose self-awareness is denied and replaced by imposed culture and morality (communism).
3. He stressed personal sacrifice, 'martyrdom' and a permanent struggle.
4. Shiism, as a political movement, is the true expression of the teachings of Islam.
5. Waiting for the reappearance of the last Imam has been used as an excuse for inaction and rigidity while it should be a period of action and preparation for the Imam's coming. Thus, this Shiah religious belief was turned into a dynamic force.
6. The *Imamah* as a concept differs from Western democracy and dictatorship since it implies a combination of theological distinction and popular support and acceptance.
7. Religious duties are a social responsibility for each Muslim and matters should not be left to religious leaders loyal to the regime.
8. Islam, Shari'ati emphasized, accorded women a positive role and they should be given the right to participate in all spheres of life.
9. He stressed the dangers of colonization of peoples' minds which results in alienation from one's own culture and identity. This alienation is a result of the importation of a foreign culture and a foreign economic system which destroys the individual's ties with his own culture and heritage.

The answer to this problem, Shari'ati argued, resides in the concept of a 'unified man'. The aim of this concept is to unify man with his ideology and cultural values. The principle of 'higher economic returns' which has governed western societies at the expense of the humanity of the individual in the advanced industrial nations led to a consumer society in the market economies, and to the creation of state capital and 'men of the state' in the planned economies. Both societies have turned man into a 'tool of production'. The 'unified man' is achieved by 'forcing the Iranian man . . . to solve his own internal contradictions, i.e. the contradiction between the man and his Islamic beliefs (his ideology), in order to consolidate or unify the Muslim and his ideology . . . [so that he becomes] capable of building a "unified society".'[14]

The crucial factors in creating the unity between man and his ideology are 'continued practice and purification'. Thus, a 'dynamic Islam' will be created whereby one can reject past circumstances, and Shiism will enable man to continually assess new issues in the light of new conditions. To be able to play this role, man has to be free to make his own decisions in life and organizational restraints must be abolished.

The above ideas and concepts reflect the influence of Western education on the Iranian intellectual. This influence has been a pervasive source of estrangement of the small segment of Western-educated Iranian intellectuals from the larger society. What Shari'ati achieved was a synthesis of Western and Shiah political and social thought that bridges this wide gulf; but it achieves this within the framework of Shiah religious doctrines as developed over centuries of political and social struggle.

Ayatollah Khomeini

Ayatollah Khomeini also emerged as a central figure in the revolution against the Shah. Although it passed largely unnoticed at the time, he was one of the first to systematically elucidate clerical opposition to Reza Shah's reforms (albeit in 1944, three years after Reza Shah's abdication).[15] He distinguished himself as a staunch, uncomprising and outspoken opponent of the regime in Iran as early as 1962. The first clash between Khomeini and the regime in Iran took place after the Iranian parliament passed a law granting Americans in Iran immunity from prosecution in Iranian courts.[16] Khomeini reacted to this angrily by saying:

If any of them commits a crime in Iran, they are immune. If an American servant or cook terrorizes your source of religious authority in the middle of the bazaar, the Iranian police does not have the right to stop him. The Iranian courts cannot put him on trial or interrogate him. He should go to America where the

masters would decide what to do . . . . We do not consider this
government a government. These are traitors. They are traitors
to the country.[17]

As a result of his fiery attack on the Shah, and of the existing
repression in Iran, Khomeini was detained for two months and then
released to be put under house arrest for four months.[18]

The second major clash between Khomeini and the authorities
pertained to the Shah's agrarian reform of 1963. Demonstrations
broke out in Iran. A group of *ulama* were killed by the Iranian police in
the Fayzieh school in Qum. Khomeini made statements condemning
the actions of the government. Following this, Khomeini was sent into
exile in Turkey and then to Iraq, where he settled in Najaf for fourteen
years. There, Khomeini continued to agitate against the Shah. Najaf is
the centre of Shiah religious studies, and Khomeini, during the years
of his exile there, had a tremendous impact on the thousands of
Iranian students of religious studies who returned to Iran armed with
his analyses of the country's problems. In October 1978 he left Iraq to
live in Paris, where he stayed until his triumphant return in February
1979.

There are striking similarities between the Iranian revolution of
1978 and the Constitutional revolution of 1905–6. The clergy again
assumed prominence, due to the fact that the secularist forces (such as
the National Front and various leftist organizations, including Tudeh),
were in a state of disarray because of the continuous pressure which
the Shah and SAVAK inflicted on these groups. The leaders of these
groups were either in jail, in exile, or dead. Urban guerrilla groups
occasionally clashed with the authorities but they were never able to
develop the mass base necessary to sustain effective guerrilla
warfare.[19] The absence of legalized independent political parties
capable of articulating the interests and political opinions of the
opposition forces made the mosque in Iran a centre for political
agitation against the Shah.

Popular discontent among the various Iranian social classes is
another common feature which contributed to the success of the clergy.
The merchants and artisans of the bazaar were very discontented
because supermarkets and factories had replaced workshops and
decreased the economic power of the bazaar. A new merchant class
with close contacts with members of the royal family emerged and was
able to import goods tax free. In combating inflation, price inspectors
and the militia of the Rastakhiz party (Shah's party) cracked down on

merchants who were not paying import duties while those with close connections with the royal family were usually left alone. Farmers were in debt with small pieces of land, a factor which forced a great number of them to migrate to the cities, where they became the downtrodden of urban life. The Shah's implementation of rapid industrialization and capital-intensive development projects, without any regard to Iranian culture and traditions, combined with the people's unwillingness to pay a high price for this mode of development, paved the way for the mass uprising in Iran.

The arrogance of government officials in dealing with the people was another factor contributing to the revolution. Oil revenues did not result in immediate benefits to the Iranian people. The top 10 per cent of the people accounted for about 40 per cent of total consumption.[20] High inflation and housing shortages forced people to pay about 50 per cent of their income on rent.[21] The clergy who 'live in real symbiosis with the Muslim masses' assumed the role of articulator and interpreter of people's aspirations in their confrontation with the Shah.[22] The imprisonment and killing of mullahs (as on 11 May 1978 in Shari'at Madari's house) represented a martyrdom of religious leaders in the political struggle with the Shah.

Another feature common to the two Iranian revolutions is the role of dominant foreign powers in Iranian internal affairs. The CIA-sponsored coup in 1953 against Mosaddeq remained in the minds of the Iranian people as an ugly reality of power politics. Hence Khomeini's continued statements about foreigners who 'do not sleep. They are making plans to resume their pillaging in other forms'.[23] The continued American support for the Shah, and the billions of dollars of arms sales to make Iran a major regional power capable of safeguarding American interests in the area, gave the opposition and Khomeini a permanent source of fuel in their attacks on the Shah and the United States. To Khomeini these weapons had 'no purpose other than to realize the plans of the American plunderers . . .; they have no purpose other than consolidating United States bases in Iran, the better to smother the resistance of the Iranian people and the other peoples of this region who are fighting against the occupiers of Palestine and against the international exploiters.'[24]

During the Carter Administration, the inconsistency of American foreign policy *vis-à-vis* the Shah became particularly acute. Publicly, Carter espoused a commitment to human rights and democratization, which entailed pressure on some US allies to liberalize their political systems. This led to high expectations in societies living under oppressive regimes, particularly in Iran. Prominent Iranians sent a memorandum to President Carter and US Representative to the United Nations Andrew Young regarding the situation in Iran. In it they requested that Richard Helms, the US Ambassador in Iran and former CIA Chief, be removed and tried for his activities in supporting the Shah and oppressing the Iranian people. They also requested a board of inquiry to be sent to Iran.[25] Open letters to the Shah started to circulate in Tehran, and committees were formed for the protection of human rights.

Despite the growth of such opposition to his regime, the Shah hesitated to act, for fear of antagonizing Carter. However, after a meeting between Carter and the Shah in 1977, a bargain was struck between the two concerning the purchase of nuclear installations and military hardware by Iran. In return, the Shah accepted a freeze on oil prices. As a result of this deal, the President of the United States, while visiting Tehran on 31 December 1977, had the audacity (or naïveté) to declare that the Shah 'shared his views on human rights'. Having achieved this 'democratic seal of approval', the Shah decided to escalate violence against the opposition and religious leaders. He ordered the publication of an article in the government press attacking Khomeini. The ultimate conclusion for all Iranians was that the United States still seemed to 'prefer strong dictatorships to constitutional monarchies'.[26] The US State Department continued to issue statements of support for the Shah, in spite of the hundreds who were being killed in Iranian cities. The last of these statements was issued in the first week of December 1978, about one month prior to the Shah's final departure from Iran. Senator Richard Lugar reflected the opinion of the majority of US government officials when he expressed his belief that the Shah would be able to survive the crisis.[27]

As a charismatic leader and religious authority, Khomeini saw himself 'empowered to act', as deaths in demonstrations acquired huge dimensions.[28] It became an act necessary for the will of God. The army could not continue killing people for ever because 'it will be absorbed by the people'. The army's repression was only 'a proof that things are going badly'.[29] Consequently, perseverance in the struggle becomes of paramount importance because, 'Life is a lesson and a struggle. And without contradiction to Muslim thought . . . death is better than a life of humiliation; no other way out but continuation of the war by every means . . . to achieve honour and glory.'[30] Resistance must be based on a long-term strategy because the establishment of an Islamic state requires 'emancipating efforts'. Immediate success should not be the prerequisite for action because 'great men plan for the next generation'.[31]

Khomeini advocated 'violent protest' to achieve the revolution. He encouraged the *ulama* and the preachers in the mosques to explain the regime's real intentions, which he believed would undoubtedly turn the Iranian people against it.[32] Telegrams of protest should be sent by all the Muslim *ulama* to corrupt and repressive regimes.[33] Propaganda work was another effective method: ideas crystallize among a group of people. Religious occasions such as *'hajj'* Friday prayers and Islamic feasts should all be used for the purposes of Islamic ideology, and to call for the unity of Muslims, as well as offering Islamic solutions to the problems of the community. Liberation of other Muslims, such as the Palestinians, should be worked for.[34]

People's discontent and resentment should also be utilized: 'People are petrified by the dictators and they need a courageous voice to represent their aspirations.'[35] Organization, planning and action are essential. Change can be realized, either by infiltrating the system or by external attack.[36]

Unity of the people is an essential condition for victory, and unity between the leadership and the people must always be maintained. Actions must reflect the needs and aspirations of the people. The leadership must always strive to raise people's awareness by explaining the legal, religious, social, economic and political solutions which Islam offers.[37] The youth must be saved from the 'imperialist attempts at corrupting them'. Propaganda work must reach university students, since they are the 'staunchest opponents of repression, despotism, treachery, agents of imperialism, and the plunderers of national wealth.'[38]

Religious institutions should be reformed, and purged of all the *ulama* who support and benefit from the regimes. These *ulama* should be uncovered because they are the enemies of Islam. Unity between religion and politics should be re-emphasized because 'imperialism brainwashed people' into believing otherwise.[39]

Passive resistance is another tactic which can be realized by:

1. Boycotting all the institutions of the despotic government.
2. Non-cooperation with it.
3. Avoiding any activity that benefits such a government.
4. Establishing alternative judicial, financial, economic, cultural and political institutions.[40]

Khomeini's theory of Islamic government

In his major treatise on Islamic government, Khomeini identified the functions of Islamic government as:

1. To enforce the laws of the *Shari'a* justly.
2. To combat oppression of the rights of ordinary individuals and to eradicate corruption.
3. To fight 'heresies and errors' that are legislated by false parliaments.
4. To prevent the intervention of foreigners in the affairs of the Muslims.[41]

The structure of government emanates directly from these essential functions. The form of Islamic government, according to Khomeini, is constitutional:

> However, it is not constitutional in the popular sense of the word which means representation in the parliamentary system or in the people's councils. It is constitutional in the sense that those in charge of affairs observe a number of conditions and rules outlied in the Qur'ān and in the Sunna.... This is why the Islamic government is the government of the Divine Law.[42]

The constitutional basis of government, then, is sacrosanct and immutable law. Thus, the traditional legislative powers of government are abrogated:

> The difference between the Islamic government and constitutional governments . . . lies in the fact that the people's representatives . . . are the ones who codify and legislate, whereas the power of legislation is confined to God . . . and no one else has the right to legislate and no one may rule by that which has not been given power by God. This is why Islam replaces the legislative council by a planning council that works to run the affairs and work of the ministries so that they may offer their services in all spheres.[43]

What is the role of a parliament, then? During the period of the Greater Occultation, Khomeini maintains, there are no specific texts on a particular person to be the ruler of the Islamic community.

Nevertheless, the necessity for government continues. 'Despite the absence of a provision designating an individual to act on behalf of the Imam in the case of his absence, the presence of the qualities of the religious ruler in any individual still qualify him to rule the people.'[44] In addition to the general requirements of intelligence, maturity and a good sense of management, there are two essential qualities of leadership: first, knowledge of Islamic law; second, justice.[45] According to Khomeini, these qualities can be found among most of the Muslim jurists (*ulama*): 'A jurist means a person knowledgeable in the Islamic creeds, laws, rules and ethics, i.e. he is a person familiar with all that the Prophet brought.'[46] The real rulers in the less than ideal state, then, are the jurists.[47] As people knowledgeable about everything that the Prophet ordained, their 'mission has been to revolt and fight against despotic regimes.'[48] The empowerment of the jurists is an essential matter that is ordained by *Shari'a*. The jurists have the same power and authority with respect to governance that the Prophet or Imams had, with one exception: since all jurists are equal, in the absence of the Imam, no one jurist can legitimately have power over other jurists. The role of parliament, although not discussed directly, appears to be as a forum for the management of doctrinal conflict among the jurists in the interpretation and application of Divine Law in the development of contemporary policies:

> The jurists must work separately or collectively to set up a legitimate government that establishes the structures, protects the borders and establishes order. If competence for this task is confined to one person, then this would be his duty to do so corporeally, otherwise the duty is shared equally. In case of difficulty in forming that government, the [attribution] to rule does not disappear. The jurists have been appointed by God to rule and the jurists must act as much as possible in accordance with their assignment . . . . The temporary inability to form a strong and complete government does not at all mean that we should retreat. Dealing with the needs of the Muslims and implementing among them whatever laws are possible to implement is a duty as much as possible.[49]

Khomeini maintained that Islamic government does not mean religious government. 'The future leaders must be engaged in defending the ideas and beliefs of the people.'[50] Since Islam has no hierarchy of religious positions, the status of jurist is informal and unofficial. Essentially, it emerges from consensus within the religious community and is closely related to the creation of a constituency within the social community. It is the religious leaders, Khomeini wrote, who represent the ideas and beliefs of the people, and they would be the first choice of the electorate in a democratic process. Nevertheless, high public office, particularly executive office, has responsibilities which require secular 'specialists capable of facing up to their jobs. For their part, the religious – with the people – will see to it that public affairs are well run, just as they have helped the people, by means of their directives, to overthrow the Shah's corrupt regime.'[51] Commenting on the tasks of public administration, Khomeini noted: 'Naturally, it is not the duty of any civil servant, whatever his task, to know all the laws and to study them deeply. It is enough for such a person to familiarize himself with the laws relevant to his functions or to the task entrusted to him.'[52]

While neither the legislative nor the executive positions of government are necessarily religious in the Islamic state, the role of the clergy as adjudicators of public affairs is a specifically religious task. Noting that 'the position of judge is exclusively for the just jurist',[53] Khomeini observed that the knowledge of Islamic law and justice are essential to the judiciary, which functions to 'dispense justice among the people'.[54] However, the role of the judiciary is not confined to the dispensing of justice. The function of the judiciary is to supervise the legislative and executive branches of government to maintain their conformity to Divine Law in the on-going affairs of society. Explaining this role, Khomeini cites a precedent in which a provincial governor inquired of the twelfth Imam, Sahib al-Zaman, about some problematical issues. Interpreting the enquiry, and the Imam's response, Khomeini maintains:

Naturally, what is meant by the intended events is not the canonical laws and issues. The inquirer knew his authority on these issues and laws. People referred to the jurists when they had a problem with any of the canonical laws and rules . . . . He was asking about the authority on the contemporary social problems and on the developments in the people's life. Because it was impossible to refer to the imam due to the latter's absence, the inquirer wanted to know the authority on the changes in life, on society's developments and on transient events and did not know what to do.[55]

It is in the judicial capacity of overseeing the constitutional legitimacy of public policy that the jurists are the rulers of the state. While public administration may be an essentially temporal task, its unity with Divine Law is maintained by the judiciary. 'If the sultans are pious at all', wrote Khomeini, 'then all they have to do is proceed in their decisions and actions on the advice of the jurists. In such a case, the real rulers are the jurists and the sultans are nothing but people working for them.'[56] This advice has two channels: through parliament, which represents the ideas and beliefs of the electorate and would presumably reflect a substantial religious orientation; and through the judiciary, which represents the intrinsic knowledge and justice of the religious community.

The nature of the just society

Intrinsic in any theory of government is the ideal of a just society. Arguing that Islam is a social system, not merely a system of worship, and that Islamic government has as its primary concern the implementation of Divine social legislation, Khomeini stated:

> The Qur'ān verses concerned with society's affairs are numerous compared to the verses concerned with private worship. In any of the detailed Hadith books, you can hardly find more than three or four sections concerned with regulating man's private worship and man's relationship with God . . . . The rest is strongly related to social and economic [affairs], with human rights, with administration and with the policy of societies.[57]

Furthermore, the purpose of the Islamic social system is the regulation of man's relationship to man for the attainment of man's mortal happiness. Only in a just society can man actively pursue his spiritual progress. The achievement of such a society is the explicit purpose of Islamic government, and has been the specific failure of the industrialized East or West:

> Let them go to Mars or anywhere they wish; they are still backward in the sphere of securing happiness to man, backward in spreading moral virtues and backward in creating a psychological and spiritual progress similar to the material progress. They are still unable to solve their social problems because solving these problems and eliminating hardship requires an ideological and moral spirit. The material gains in the sphere of

overcoming nature and invading the space cannot accomplish this task. Wealth, capabilities and resources require the Islamic faith, creed and ethics to become complete and balanced, to serve man to avert him from injustice and poverty. We alone possess such beliefs, morals and laws. We should not cast aside our religion and laws just because somebody goes to the moon or makes something. These laws are directly related to man's life; they carry the nucleus of reforming society and securing happiness in this world and in the hereafter.[58]

What is the nature of Khomeini's professed just society? It is a society where economic power is distinctly separated from political power. It is the linkage of economic and political power that makes government an end in itself. 'Governing is not an end in itself', Khomeini maintains. 'If sought as a goal and if all means are used to attain it, then it degenerates to the level of a crime and its seekers come to be considered criminals.'[59] Government has no right to arbitrarily undermine the private property of individuals.[60] It only has those rights to taxation of profits already legislated for in the Qur'ān, and it is the duty of an Islamic government to ensure that this law is applied without privilege or discrimination. Therefore, the accumulation of material wealth is not proscribed. However, the taxation system and the alms system legislated for in the Qur'ān guarantee that there will not be exaggerations of either wealth or poverty, and the legal system guarantees that wealth is not secured through exploitation.

How is the separation of economic and political power to be maintained? By ensuring that political office does not result in privilege, favour or material gain. The holders of political office must live humbly and piously.[61] Khomeini considers the accumulation of material gain and conspicuous consumption the most manifest indicators of political corruption.[62] Since political office is a task, not a privilege, it is incumbent upon politicians to emulate the Prophet and pious Imams in their lifestyle:

> The life of the great Prophet was a life of utter simplicity, even though the Prophet was the head of the state who headed it, directed it and ruled it by himself. This method continued to a degree after him and until the Ummayads seized power. The government of 'Ali ibn Talib was a government of reform, as you know, and 'Ali lived a life of utter simplicity while managing a vast state.... I do not believe the poor people can live the kind of

life that the Imam lived . . . . You know that most of the corrupt aspects of our society are due to the corruption of the ruling dynasty and the royal family. What is the legitimacy of these rulers who build houses of entertainment, corruption, fornication and abomination . . .?[63]

While wealth is not an evil in itself (although unjust profit is an 'abominable sin'),[64] the social welfare system established in Islam which mandates government protection of the rights and needs of the underprivileged, together with the tax system, provides a fundamental framework for redistribution of wealth and guarantees social equity. Through this system, Khomeini maintains, 'Islam solved the problem of poverty'.[65] This system provides the basic social policy of an Islamic government. It established human need, not greed, as the link between politics and economics. 'Provisions of the Islamic canonical law', argues Khomeini, 'contain various laws for a complete social system. Under this system, all of man's needs are met.'[66]

The just society, then, is the society where Divine Law is implemented without privilege or discrimination – a society where both the transgressor and the transgressed are secure in their knowledge of swift, equitable application of the law.[67] It is axiomatic that God's Law is inherently just. It is man's interpretation and application of the law that leads to injustice. This must be guarded against in the structure of government during the period of absence. It is in this period that the danger that 'laws and rules would be changed and the heretics would add to them and the atheists would detract from them' is great.[68] Furthermore, Khomeini maintains, 'We have found people to be deficient and imperfect, regardless of their inclinations and their various states.'[69] Hence, Islamic government in the period of absence must provide a system of checks and balances to fallible human interpretation and application of the Divine Law, indeed to fallible human nature:

> If we [the *ulama*] want to immortalize the rules of the Shari'a in practice, to prevent violation of the rights of weak people, to prevent corruption on earth, to apply the Shari'a laws justly, to fight the heresies and the deviations decided upon by the sham parliaments and to prevent the influence and intervention of the enemies in the affairs of the Muslims, we [the *ulama*] must form the government because all this is carried out by a government led by a trustworthy, and pious ruler who commits no injustice, deviation or corruption.[70]

Constructing the Islamic Republic

Although Khomeini's views regarding the nature and structure of Islamic government represent the most comprehensive and important treatment of this topic within Shiah political thought since Mizra Muhammad Husayn Na'ini, other prescriptions for Islamic government were produced in the course of the struggle against the Shah. Among these, the views of Abol-Hassan Bani-Sadr are of significant interest, given the subsequent history of the Islamic Republic of Iran.

According to Bani-Sadr, the limitations of contemporary political systems can be found in the divisions that they foster in society: divisions of class, race and nationality; division between religion and state, etc. All these divisions are myths, which facilitate exploitation and violate the essential unity of God.[71] Islam, and the unity inherent therein, is the way to liberate man from such divisions.[72]

Islamic government is defined in terms of those characteristics rejected and adopted by it. Islamic government rejects social and international relations based on dominance; it refuses to use and modify Islam in the interests of power; it values self-criticism; it rejects cults of personality; it refuses to accept the principle that ends justify means.[73] Government by dominance is replaced by spiritual leadership.[74] An Islamic government must remove itself from foreign, dominating influences, and must commit itself to global liberation: 'We will not attack foreigners, but we will participate in the struggle for freedom anywhere, in accordance with the principles of holy struggle. We will assist in any way we can other movements formed to free nations from domination. Every action to liberate others corresponds with our principles.'[75]

Bani-Sadr placed considerable emphasis on the need to devolve political power to the people: '... we must return power from the top to the base, the masses, to whom the power originally belonged. So long as there are power centres, power cannot be distributed throughout society.'[76] He enumerated several specific executive safeguards which should be implemented in an Islamic government so as to diminish the possibility of a return to dominating rule. A popular army must be formed which could defend the nation without becoming a possible power centre.[77] Economic safeguards should be implemented whereby consumption patterns were controlled and 'anything which sets one individual above others, whether in the way of food or clothing, is forbidden.'[78] The political leadership of the Islamic government must be subject to public supervision through mass political participation, criticism and consultation.[79] Islamic government demands that '... everyone of its members becomes a spiritual struggler and a religious scholar, [so that] no one needs to ask another what he must do, because such would result in a religious dictatorship.'[80]

The differences between Bani-Sadr's view of Islamic government, with its emphasis on the devolution of power to the masses, and Khomeini's view of Islamic government, which demands allegiance to the Islamic jurists, are clear enough. But these differences were submerged as both men fought Pahlavi rule from exile in Paris. Following the overthrow of the Shah, however, differences regarding the nature of government came to the fore as the leaders of the revolution sought to construct an Islamic Republic in Iran.

The first indication of the shape of things to come arose with the emergence of a new Iranian Constitution in December 1979.[81] Despite provisions for an elected presidency and National Consultative Assembly, the Constitution vested paramount power in a 'leader' or 'leadership council', the requirements of which were 'the necessary competence in theology and piety to deliver formal opinions and authority'.[82] The leader or leadership council were given a vast array of powers, including the power to appoint the senior judiciary; command of the armed forces; and final approval over presidential candidates. The first leader was to be Ayatollah Khomeini.[83]

Directly below the leader is a twelve-man Council of Guardians. Six members of this Council are religious jurists, appointed by the leadership. These members vet all laws passed by the National Consultative Assembly so as to assure their conformity with Islam. The full Council of Guardians vets constitutional law, interprets the Constitution, and oversees elections to the presidency and National Consultative Assembly.[84]

The form of government outlined in the Iranian Constitution thus adhered to the clerically-directed model expounded by Khomeini – a point acknowledged in the Constitution's preamble:

> So as to assure the permanent security of the Constitution, the rights of clerical leadership is [sic] under all conditions to be the leadership recognized by the people. (The course of affairs is in the hands of those who know God and who are trustworthy in matters having to do with what He permits and forbids.)
>
> The just jurist is equipped to ensure that the various organizations do not deviate from their true Islamic duties.[85]

The preamble also acknowledges that the 'plan of Islamic government is based on religious authority which was introduced by Imam Khomeini'.

Abol-Hassan Bani-Sadr was subsequently elected first President of the Islamic Republic of Iran in January 1980. Thereafter, the fundamental incompatibility of these two views of Islamic government manifested itself in the form of ideological and political conflict between Bani-Sadr and his supporters on the one hand, and elements of the clergy organized into the Islamic Republican Party and led by Ayatollah Beheshti on the other. This latter group had the tacit, and later open, support of Ayatollah Khomeini. Ultimately, Bani-Sadr's forces were defeated, and the President was forced from power and into exile in 1981. Once more in Paris, Bani-Sadr joined with Mujahidin-Khalq leader Mas'od Rajavi in forming the Council for the National Resistance Front, an organization opposed to Khomeini's rule. At that time Bani-Sadr issued a statement condemning political repression and dictatorship in Iran:

> [Before the Revolution] it was accepted that in Islam it is not the individual who governs but the law. Based on this, it was considered obvious that if the implementation of Islamic law were safeguarded, the government of individuals merely because they belonged to a special stratum would be unnecessary.
> ... In this republic – as the abolition of dictatorship was accepted in the course of the Islamic revolution and since the Constitutional Revolution – any kind of guardianship can only be implemented through a public vote and the free will of the people of the country.[86]

Bani-Sadr's plea for Islamic democracy was not the only opposition to the move towards Khomeini's model of government that emerged from within the Iranian revolution. Some of the clergy themselves opposed the concentration of executive powers in clerical hands, arguing that the genuine implementation of the *Shari'a* must await the reappearance of the hidden Imam.[87]

Conclusion

The manifestation of Islamic government in Iran is both the product of an intellectual tradition and of a particular set of political and social forces – some common to Muslim culture and some specific to Iran.

While Shiah political thought developed in response to Iran's political and social problems, it is important to point out the significant social role of Islamic theoretical and intellectual inquiry in Islamic societies. The social role of religious theory contrasts sharply with that of scientific theory. The mystifying role of abstract scientific theory makes philosophic and/or theoretical inquiry accessible only to specialized elites and is beyond the masses, being largely irrelevant as a problem-solving approach to their day-to-day dilemmas. In contrast, the nature, meanings and relevance of Islamic theoretical and intellectual inquiry have been carried directly to the people through the central social role of the *ulama* and the mosque. In Islamic societies, the mosque functions as a formal and informal gathering place where the *ulama* are in close contact with the problems and sufferings of their communities and where they make Islamic thought a relevant, unified problem-solving approach to personal and public, individual and community dilemmas. Where, as in Iran under the Shah, the mosque is the only institution for the expression of public opinion that has not been driven underground or eliminated completely by political oppression, the central dilemmas facing Islamic theory are public ones and the role of the mosque and the *ulama* is politicized. However, where the mosque becomes part of the formal political institution and the *ulama* are agents of the state, as in Iran under Khomeini's Islamic government, the socio-political relationship between community and *ulama* is transformed into a power relationship. Furthermore, Islamic theory – an ideology of revolution under the Shah – has become state doctrine under Khomeini's Islamic regime. There is a substantial disjuncture between the paradigms of state Islam and the ideologies of revolutionary Islam, as discussed in Chapter 6.

Notes

1. See Abdul-Hadi Hairi, *Shiism and Constitutionalism in Iran*, Leiden, E.J. Brill, 1977, pp. 55–65. See also Hamid Algar, *Religion and State in Iran, 1785–1906*, Berkeley, University of California Press, 1969, pp. 1–25.
2. Azar Tabari, 'Role of the Shi'i Clergy in Modern Iranian Politics', *Khamsin* 9, 1981, p. 51.
3. Quoted in Hairi, op. cit., p.99.
4. Ibid., pp. 100–1.
5. Ibid., p. 166.
6. Ibid., pp. 168–82.
7. Quoted in ibid., p. 189.
8. Quoted in ibid., p. 191.
9. Ibid., p. 194.

10. Ibid., p. 213.
11. Tabari, op cit., pp. 61–2.
12. Ibid., p. 66.
13. See Hamid Algar, trans., *On the Sociology of Islam: Lectures by Ali Shari'ati*, Berkeley, Mizan Press, 1980 and R. Campbell, trans., *Marxism and Other Western Fallacies*, Berkeley, Mizan Press, 1980 for the only works of Shari'ati widely available in English. For interpretive accounts of Shari'ati's writings and role in the revolution, see Michel Noufel, 'Al-Nahar's Analysis From Teheran', *Al-Nahar*, Beirut, 24 February 1979; Yann Richard, 'Ali Shari'ati, the Precursor', *Nouvelles Littéraires*, Paris, 7–14 December 1978, pp. 24–5; Ervand Abrahamian, 'Ali Shari'ati: Ideologue of the Iranian Revolution', Merip Reports, January 1982, pp. 25–8. Also see Gilles Auquetil, 'Interview with Daryush Shayegan', in *Nouvelles Litéraires*, op. cit., pp. 26–33.
14. Michel Noufel, *Al-Nahar*, Beirut, 25 February 1979.
15. Tabari, op. cit., p. 62.
16. Thiery A. Brun, 'Resurgence of Popular Agitation in Iran', *Le Monde Diplomatique*, Paris, July 1978.
17. 'History of Khomeyni's Leadership Given', *Ettela'at*, Tehran, 1 February 1979.
18. *Tehran Journal*, 16 January 1979.
19. See Fred Halliday, *Iran: Dictatorship and Development*, Middlesex, Penguin Books, 1979, pp. 211–48.
20. Ibid., p. 15.
21. 'Analysis of Recent Disturbances', *Masa' El-E Jahan*, Tehran, September/October 1978.
22. *Le Monde Diplomatique*, Paris, December 1978.
23. Quoted by Morteza Kotobi and Jean Leon in 'The March Towards the Islamic Republic of Iran: Society and Religion According to Imam Khomeini', *Le Monde Diplomatique*, Paris, April 1979.
24. 'Imam Khomeyni Versus Imperialism, Zionism, Reactionism', pamphlet published or distributed by Éditions Abu Dhar, Paris.
25. Among the authors of the report was Mozaffar Firouz, former minister and vice president of Iran's Council of Ministers. 'Is the Shah "Unaccountable"?', *Le Monde Diplomatique*, Paris, 27 July 1978. Helms was eventually removed from his position. He subsequently became an adviser to the Shah.
26. Brun, op. cit., p. 60. Similar American inconsistencies were demonstrated during the administration of John F. Kennedy, who pushed for a programme of reform in Iran before giving the Shah a $35m US loan. But this condition was sacrificed after the major rebellion led by the *ulama* in the period 1962–63. For further details, see Halliday, op. cit., pp. 26–7.
27. 'Struggle for Power Likely to be Protracted', *Al-Nahar Arab Report and Memo*, 11 December 1978, pp. 5–7. This article also includes the position of other western powers *vis-à-vis* the Shah. For a summarized account of Iran's foreign relations with major Western powers, the Soviet Union and China, see Halliday, op.cit., the chapter on foreign relations.
28. Quoted by Kotobi and Leon, op. cit., p. 83.
29. Ibid., p. 83.

30. 'Imam Khomeyni Versus Imperialism', op. cit., p. 2.
31. Ayatollah al-Khomeini, *Al-Hukuma al-Islamiyah* (Islamic Government), Beirut, Dar al-Tali'ah lil taba'ah wa-al-Nashir, 2nd edn, 1979.
32. 'Imam Khomeyni Versus Imperialism', op. cit., p. 12.
33. Ayatollah al-Khomeini, op. cit., p. 112.
34. Ibid., pp. 125–6.
35. Ibid., p. 127.
36. Ibid., p. 119.
37. Ibid., pp. 119–20.
38. Ibid., pp. 122–3.
39. Ibid., pp. 132–45.
40. Ibid., pp. 132–45. See also 'Imam Khomeyni Versus Imperialism', op. cit., p. 8.
41. *Islamic Government*, op. cit., p. 39.
42. Ibid., p. 41.
43. Ibid.
44. Ibid., p. 48.
45. Ibid., pp. 43–8.
46. Ibid., p. 76.
47. Ibid., p. 46.
48. Ibid., p. 76. See also 'Imam Khomeyni Versus Imperialism', op. cit., p. 7.
49. Ibid., p. 51.
50. *Le Nouvel Économiste*, 29 January 1979, p. 30.
51. Ibid.
52. *Islamic Government*, op. cit., p. 46.
53. Ibid., p. 74.
54. Ibid., p. 75.
55. Ibid., p. 77.
56. Ibid., p. 42.
57. *Islamic Government*, op. cit., p. 9.
58. Ibid., pp. 17–18.
59. Ibid., p. 53.
60. Ibid., pp. 70–1.
61. Ibid., pp. 43, 47.
62. Ibid., pp. 107–8.
63. Ibid., pp. 43, 44.
64. Ibid., p. 107.
65. Ibid., p. 114.
66. Ibid., p. 27.
67. Ibid., pp. 70–2.
68. Ibid., p. 38.
69. Ibid.
70. Ibid., p. 39.
71. Abol-Hassan Bani-Sadr, *The Fundamental Principles and Precepts of Islamic Government*, trans. Mohammed G. Ghanoonparvar, Lexington, Kentucky, Mazda Publishers, 1981, pp. 19–23.
72. Ibid., pp. 37–8.
73. Ibid., pp. 59–64.
74. Ibid., pp. 64–5.

75. Ibid., p. 71.
76. Ibid., p. 69.
77. Ibid., pp. 75–8.
78. Ibid., p. 79.
79. Ibid., pp. 78–9.
80. Ibid., p. 14.
81. 'The Constitution of the Islamic Republic of Iran' can be found in T.Y. Ismael, *Iran and Iraq: Roots of Conflict*, Syracuse, Syracuse University Press, 1982, pp. 142–86.
82. Article 109 of the Constitution.
83. Articles 107, 110, op. cit.
84. Articles 91–9, op. cit.
85. Preamble to the Constitution.
86. 'A Covenant of the Council for the National Resistance Front' in Abol-Hassan Bani-Sadr, op. cit., pp. 96–7.
87. Enver M. Koury, 'The Ayatollah Revolution: Lack of Consensus on Fundamentals', in Enver M. Koury and Charles G. MacDonald (eds), *Revolution in Iran: A Reappraisal*, Hyattsville, Maryland, Institute of Middle Eastern and North African Affairs, 1982, p. 74.

5 Contemporary Islamic Political Activism: Egypt*

Despite many years of underground political activity by Islamic groups in Egypt, it was not until the Iranian revolution (1979) and the assassination of Egyptian President Anwar al-Sadat (October 1981) that significant attention was directed towards them by analysts outside the country. In the 1980s, however, there has been a veritable avalanche of literature on Islamic political activism in Egypt and the Arab world. Much of this literature has attributed the growth of contemporary Islamic militancy to ideological influences from Iran – 'Khomeinism' – with Egypt being portrayed as one potentially rich 'breeding ground' for such Iranian-sponsored/inspired fanaticism.[1] In the Western popular press in particular, the dominant metaphor for the growth of contemporary Islamic political activism in the Middle East became a quasi-medical one, with moderate (pro-Western) regimes subject to a fundamentalist infection of alien origin.

As the previous chapters indicate, such an assessment is inaccurate. The Islamic groups politically active in Egypt are the product of indigenous development, a fact made clear by even a cursory examination of their ideological and organizational development. Whereas Iran's Islamic revolution drew its strength and ideology from centuries of Shiite opposition to the status quo within Islam, Egypt's contemporary Islamic revolutionaries looked to the local and much more recent example of the Muslim Brotherhood for lessons. Instead of representing the by-products of an Islamic revolution in Iran, Islamic activist groups in Egypt are better seen as a similar but separate reaction to a socio-political environment characterized by gross inequalities in power and wealth, unmet social and political expectations, and a continued pattern of foreign dependence and influence. In Egypt, as in Iran, such social problems prompted a significant (albeit much smaller) segment of the population to find their explanation in

* The authors wish to acknowledge the collaboration of Rex Brynen in the preparation of this chapter.

deviation from the path of Islam, and hence to advocate the 're-Islamification' of society as their only possible solution.

Whatever the broad parallels between the Iranian and Egyptian cases, examination of the particular and specific conditions of the latter is vital to any analysis of the growth of contemporary Islamic political activism in Egypt. Indeed, five developments in Egyptian society and politics can be shown to have had a considerable impact on this growth: the June 1967 defeat, the limitations of Nasser's socialism, Sadat's encouragement of Islamic political forces, the social costs of Sadat's *infitah* (open-door) economic policy, and Egypt's political realignment with the West.

The June 1967 defeat

The overwhelming Arab defeat in the June 1967 Arab–Israeli war sent a shock wave through the Arab world. The shock was particularly acute in Egypt, which not only lost territory to enemy occupation but also (and perhaps more importantly) saw its post-1952 role of leadership and mission under Nasser dealt a serious blow. In the re-examination and introspection which followed the June 1967 defeat, two major streams of Arab political thought emerged. The first of these, offered by the Arab New Left, held that the Arab world's failure was due to inadequate social mobilization and the continued presence of dysfunctional and oppressive social structures. According to the New Left, victory could only be achieved with the socialist transformation of Arab society.[2]

The second stream of thought to emerge from the wreckage of June 1967 was that of resurgent Islamic political activism. Proponents of this view argued that failure was attributable to the godless and secular features of the Arab states. According to this stream of thought, only when these states and their people returned to the laws and tenets of Islam would success be achieved.

The limitations of Nasserism

In Egypt the New Left response to the June 1967 defeat was co-opted by Nasserism, which (since 1961) had advocated a socialist solution to the problems of exploitation, inequality and foreign domination. Nasser's Arab Socialist Union – the sole recognized party in Egypt from 1962 until after Nasser's death in 1970 – thus represented the official standard-bearer of socialism in Egypt.

There can be little doubt that the socialist measures introduced by Nasser – particularly in the area of land reform – contributed to a substantial reduction in the profound socio-economic inequalities in Egypt. However, the unpopular by-products of socialist transformation were a massive growth in public bureaucracy, tight controls on political participation, and the suppression of political opposition. In addition, Nasser's heavy commitment to foreign policy issues placed a substantial burden on Egypt's limited resources. In spite of these limitations, however, Nasser's regime continued to enjoy the unqualified support of the masses.

After Nasser's death in 1970, Anwar al-Sadat capitalized on these limitations to discredit Nasserism in general, and Nasser's socialist reforms in particular, thereby hoping to justify his complete reversal of Nasser's basic internal and external policies. In the reaction he unleashed, all the elements disadvantaged by Nasser's socialist experiment were encouraged to come to the fore in Egyptian politics.

Sadat's encouragement of Islamic elements

With the death of Nasser in September 1970, Vice-President Anwar al-Sadat rapidly assumed leadership of the country. Sadat soon found that many left-leaning members of the government and Arab Socialist Union opposed his ascension to power, notably former Vice-President and former Premier Ali Sabri. In May 1971 Sabri and a number of other important political figures were accused of plotting to overthrow Sadat, and were subsequently sentenced to long prison terms. Nasserites and other leftist elements (particularly those kown to be sympathetic to Ali Sabri) within the government, the Arab Socialist Union and the official press, were demoted or removed from their posts. Nasser, and many of his socialist policies, were subjected to cautious criticism. Furthermore, Sadat encouraged the growth of Islamic forces in the country as a counterweight to his socialist opponents, and increasingly sought to use Islam as a legitimizing tool for his regime. The growth of Islamic *jama'at* (groups) in Egyptian universities was encouraged by the government after May 1971. The Muslim Brotherhood, though not formally legalized, was allowed to reappear and propagate its message through the publications *al-Da'wa* and *al-I'tisam*.[3] Islamic law (the *Shari'a*) was declared to be one of the sources of legislation in the 1971 Egyptian Constitution, and eight years later the Constitution was amended so as to make the *Shari'a the main* source of legislation. In his speeches and statements Sadat replaced the nationalist symbols and socialist appeal that were the ideological foundation of Nasser's era with religious symbols and Qur'ānic invocations.[4]

Having encouraged the emergence and growth of Islamic political elements, Sadat found himself unable to control them. The Islamic *jama'at* and the Muslim Brotherhood grew increasingly critical of Sadat's foreign (rapprochement with the United States, peace with Israel) and domestic (economic conditions, inadequate democratization, deviation from Islam) policy as the 1970s progressed. Furthermore, these groups expanded in size and popular support. The circulation of *al-Da'wa*, *al-I'tisam* and other religious publications increased steadily.[5] After 1975, the university-based Islamic *jama'at* won massive victories in student union elections. In 1978, for example, its candidates won 210 out of 218 seats in Alexandria University's Faculties of Medicine, Engineering, Law and Pharmacy.[6]

These criticisms and popular electoral gains were viewed with alarm by Sadat, particularly in the aftermath of the Iranian revolution. Thus, a presidential decree was issued in 1979 dissolving the Islamic *jama'at*-dominated student unions. Later, during the large-scale arrest of Sadat's political opponents which took place in September 1981, *al-Da'wa* was suppressed and many members of the Muslim Brotherhood (including *al-Da'wa* Editor and Muslim Brotherhood leader Umar al-Tilmisani) arrested.

The social costs of infitah

Infitah – the 'open door' economic policy introduced in Egypt in 1974 – was one of the major dimensions of Sadat's reversal of Nasser's policies. *Infitah* removed virtually all restrictions on foreign capital in Egypt in the hope of attracting substantial foreign investment in Egyptian economic development. Tremendous amounts of capital were in fact attracted, but they made little real contribution to long-term productive development.[7]

The vast amount of capital influx did have profound social consequences, however.[8] The deregulation of the market which accompanied foreign aid injections (the primary source of foreign capital input) attracted foreign enterprise and stimulated the development of local private business in competition for foreign aid dollars. A distinct urban social strata emerged around the foreign aid industry, fostering the growth of an import-dependent consumer industry. This in turn contributed to the over-stimulation of the foreign goods consumer market in Egypt, leading to the 'Westernization' of the consumer market in Egypt, to the detriment of local goods and services.

Moreover, during 1975 and 1976, Egypt found itself under pressure from Arab and Western creditors to further improve the attractiveness of its economy to foreign capital by curtailing government spending and devaluing the Egyptian pound. When the Egyptian government eventually agreed to some such measures in January 1977 and reduced subsidies on over two dozen essential commodities (including rice, sugar, gasoline and cooking fuel), major riots erupted throughout Egypt, in which seventy people died and over 1,200 were arrested.[9] Although blame for the January riots was subsequently placed on the left, militant Islamic groups were also known to have taken part.[10]

A final feature of *infitah* – and one closely linked to the above dimensions – was the drain on Egyptian labour to the Arab oil-producing states. By 1978 it was estimated that over 1.3 million Egyptians were working outside the country. Furthermore, Egypt had become increasingly dependent on the remittances from this migrant labour force.[11]

While the bulk of the Egyptian population saw few, if any, of the benefits of Sadat's economic policy, a privileged minority profited tremendously from *infitah*. There was a dramatic growth in the wealthy strata of Egyptian society – from 500 millionaires in 1975 to a reported 17,000 in 1981.[12] This conspicuously wealthy and powerful Egyptian bourgeoisie, enriched by the proceeds of increased economic contact with the West, became a new force in Egyptian politics. With their growth, the level and extent of corruption apparent in Egyptian society also expanded. This contrasted sharply with the pauperization of the urban middle classes, particularly public sector employees, who found their standard of living eroded by inflation and who were rendered increasingly dependent upon government subsidies. It also contrasted with the vassalization of the peasant population as agricultural land distribution and production were deregulated.[13] Furthermore, *infitah* brought with it an inrush of Western ideas and materialism which threatened to swamp the traditional values of the (Muslim) Egyptian masses. It was in response to such alienation, and in defence of traditional values, that a significant number of (primarily young and lower middle-class) Egyptian Muslims turned to neo-activist Islam.

Sadat's realignment with the West

A fifth factor which accelerated the growth of militant Islam in Egypt was that country's rapprochement with the West and separate peace agreement with Israel. Sadat, long distrustful of the Soviet Union, and faced with an ailing economy and an inconclusive struggle with Israel, sought relief through a realignment of his country's foreign policy, away from Nasser's emphasis on anti-imperialism and Arab nationalism and towards the United States in particular. Egypt's close ties with the Soviet Union were reduced in order to accommodate the establishment of close ties with the West (particularly the United States). Furthermore, Egypt abandoned its commitment to a unified Arab struggle against Israel and sought instead a separate peace under the auspices of the United States.

The first stage of this – Egypt's move away from the Soviet Union – was welcomed by Islamic militants, who opposed friendly relations with the USSR on religious grounds. Later stages, however, met with strong disapproval. Sadat's 'peace initiative' – beginning with his 1977 trip to Jerusalem and culminating in the 1979 Camp David agreements – was portrayed by Islamic neo-activists (and much of the Arab world) as a treasonous strategy which left the holy city of Jerusalem unliberated and benefited only Zionist Israel. This view gained even more currency after 1979, when it became apparent that Israel was unwilling to return occupied territories other than the Sinai. Sadat's willingness to perform the role of staunch US ally in the region – a willingness demonstrated by military aid and co-operation – further aggravated dissatisfaction with the direction of Egypt's foreign policy. To Egypt's Islamic militants, this willingness was typified by Sadat's strong opposition to the Iranian revolution, and his offer of sanctuary to (his close friend) the Shah of Iran.

Thus, the stage was set for the growth of political activism among Islamic groups in Egypt. Sadat's foreign and domestic policies created widespread alienation from his regime. Furthermore, the internal power struggle of 1970–71 had led to growing stress on Islamic themes and state encouragement of Islamic organizations, as well as the destruction of a leftist alternative. It was therefore only natural that an Islamic critique of the status quo would emerge and win support in Egypt.

The substance of this neo-activist Islamic critique owes much to the Muslim Brotherhood. Although the contemporary Muslim Brotherhood has been criticized by Egyptian Islamic militants for its gradualist tactics (i.e. its rejection of violent confrontation and its willingness to seek partial compromise with the regime in the 1970s in exchange for quasi-legality), its analysis of Egyptian society is generally accepted. Indeed, two years of interviews with jailed militants led Egyptian sociologist Saad Eddin Ibrahim to conclude:

> In terms of the religious component of their ideology, their reading of history, and their overall vision for the future,

members of [Egypt's activist Islamic groups] expressed no differences with the Moslem Brotherhood. In fact, they considered themselves a natural continuation of the Brotherhood, which was banned and persecuted by both the Royalist regime before 1952 and by Nasser's regime after 1952. [The activist groups] revere the founder of the Brotherhood, Hassan al-Banna, and the pioneers who gave their lives as martyrs for Islam.[14]

The principle of revolution inherent in the theory and practice of contemporary Egyptian Islamic political activism does not have its roots in the mainstream of the Muslim Brotherhood represented by Hassan al-Banna, however. Instead, it owes much to the writings of Sayyid Qutb, a radical Muslim Brethren executed by Nasser's regime in 1966, whose socio-economic doctrines have been encountered in an earlier chapter. It was Qutb who interpreted Islam as a revolutionary ideology which justifies – indeed, obliges – Muslims to struggle against 'godless' social and political structures. Qutb's contribution to the ideology of neo-activist Islam deserves further examination.

The revolutionary thought of Sayyid Qutb

Central to the political thought of Sayyid Qutb (as expressed in his major political work, *Ma'lim fi al-Tariq*)[15] was the concept of *Jahiliyyah* (Ignorance of the Divine Guidance). This term, usually used to refer to the faithlessness of pre-Islamic Arabia, was employed by Qutb to refer to those aspects of modern social and political life which do not strictly conform to the teachings and principles of Islam. In particular, Qutb condemned secularism and what he saw as man's attempt to usurp God's exclusive right to define humanity's values and social system:

> This Jahiliyyah is based on rebellion against God's sovereignty on Earth. It transfers to man one of the greatest attributes of God, namely sovereignty, and makes some men lords over others. It is now not in that simple and primitive form of the ancient Jahiliyyah, but takes the form of claiming that the right to create values, to legislate rules of collective behaviour, and to choose any way of life, rests with men, without regard to what God has prescribed. The result of this rebellion against the authority of God is the oppression of his creatures. Thus the humiliation of

the common man under the communist systems and the exploitation of individuals and nations due to the greed for wealth and imperialism under the capitalist system are but a corollary of rebellion against God's authority and the denial of the dignity of man given to him by God.[16]

Qutb saw *Jahiliyyah* as extending into almost all aspects of modern life, including people's beliefs and ideas, habits, art, rules and law, to the extent that 'even what we consider to be Islamic culture, Islamic sources, Islamic philosophy, and Islamic thought are constructs of Jahiliyyah.'[17] Thus, Qutb condemned even supposedly 'Muslim' societies as being steeped in the godlessness of Jahiliyyah.

Qutb's rejection and condemnation of *jahili* society was necessarily coupled with an advocacy of society based on Islam. Islam alone provides the totality of social guidance and teaching required for righteousness and freedom from human oppression:

Islam's way of life is unique, for in systems other than Islam, some people worship others in some form or another. Only in the Islamic way of life do all men become free from the servitude of some men to others and devote themselves to the worship of God alone, deriving guidance from Him alone, and bowing before Him alone.[18]

Qutb therefore calls for Islam to assume a position of world leadership. This cannot occur if Islam is understood merely as a theory; rather, it must find concrete expression in the form of an Islamic nation within which faith –rather than race, nationality, colour, etc. – represents the criterion of membership.[19] The *Shari'a*, as laws given to man by God, represent the exclusive moral-juridical basis of such an Islamic state, and are a necessary condition for its existence. According to Qutb, adherence to the *Shari'a* is not only a matter of religious devotion, but also a practical imperative. Man, unable to comprehend the complexity and totality of the universe, is incapable of making rules for a harmonious life. Only God has this capacity, and has done so in the form of the *Shari'a*.[20]

In his writings, Sayyid Qutb placed particular emphasis on the dichotomy between Islam and the *Jahiliyyah*, between Dar al-Islam (the land of Islam) and Dar al-Harb (the land of war, i.e. the non-Islamic world). In the struggle for righteousness there is no place for blurred views regarding good and evil:

In the world there is only one party; all others are parties of Satan and rebellion . . .[21]

There is only one way to reach God; all other ways do not lead to him . . . .[22]

There is only one law which ought to be followed, and that is the Shari'a from God . . .[23]

Qutb argues that Islam, as the truth, is indivisible. It cannot be mixed or melded with non-Islamic *jahili* ideas.[24] Furthermore, his dichotomous world view leads him to warn of 'the ultimate aim of the Jews and Christians against Moslems'.[25]

Revolutionary thought must necessarily consist of three core aspects: an analysis of society's existing ills; a vision of a brighter future; and advocacy of purposive action to transform the former into the latter. The first and second of these aspects can be found in Qutb's view of *jahili* society and Islamic society respectively. It is, however, the third revolutionary aspect of Sayyid Qutb's thought – his call for *Jihad* (holy struggle) against the modern *jahiliyyah* – which has had the most significant impact on neo-activist Islam in Egypt.

According to Qutb, 'the foremost duty of Islam in this world is to depose *Jahiliyyah* from the leadership of man, and to take the leadership into its own hands and enforce the way of life which is its permanent feature'.[26] Since Muslim leaders who do not implement Islamic laws are to be considered illegitimate rulers ruling by the laws of *Jahiliyyah*, they too were to be opposed and deposed uncompromisingly. Qutb stressed that the *Jihad* of true Muslims against the *Jahiliyyah* was not an attempt to impose (Islamic) belief by force. Rather, it was the struggle to destroy those *jahili* structures which interfered with the individual's ability to embrace God through the path of Islam.[27]

Qutb envisaged the struggle against the *Jahiliyyah* being led by a small but expanding core of believers:

. . . it is necessary that there should be a vanguard which sets out with . . . determination and then keeps walking the path, marching through the vast ocean of Jahiliyyah which has encompassed the entire world. During its course, it should keep itself somewhat aloof from this all-encompassing Jahiliyyah and should also keep some ties with it. It is necessary that this vanguard should know the landmarks and milestones of the road toward this goal so that they may recognize the starting place, the nature, the responsibilities, and the ultimate purpose of this long journey. Not only this, but they also ought to be aware of their position *vis-à-vis* this jahiliyyah which has struck its stakes throughout the earth – when to cooperate with others and when to separate from them; what characteristics and qualities they should cultivate, and with what characteristics and qualities the jahiliyyah, immediately surrounding them, is armed; how to address the people of jahiliyyah in the language of Islam, and what topics and problems ought to be discussed, and when and how to obtain guidance in these matters.[28]

In other words, Qutb, while totally rejecting modern *jahili* society, called for a complete understanding of its foundations in order to combat it, not only by force, but also by refuting its arguments and exposing its shortcomings. At the same time, the faithful were to offer in the place of *Jahiliyyah* its immediate and only alternative: Islam.

Contemporary militant Islamic activism in Egypt

Sayyid Qutb's call for an Islamic vanguard was not to go unanswered. Several years after his death, a number of underground neo-activist Islamic groups arose within Egypt. Some of these, such as the group known an Jund Allah (the Soldiers of God), had only a small membership and made little significant impact on Egyptian politics and society. Others, notably Munazzamat al-Tahrir al-Islami (the Islamic Liberation Organization), Jama'at al-Musilmin (the Group of Muslims) and al-Jihad (Holy Struggle), did represent a significant force within the country. Accordingly, it is to an examination of these latter three organizations that we now turn.

The Islamic Liberation Organization (Munazzamat al-Tahrir al-Islami)[29]

The Islamic Liberation Organization was formed by Dr Salih Siriyya, a Palestinian-born Iraqi citizen with a doctorate in science education. Siriyya was a former member of the Islamic Liberation Party in Jordan.[30] After 1967 he joined a number of Palestinian organizations, and attempted to co-operate with Iraq, Libya and other 'revolutionary' Arab regimes. In 1971 he moved to Cairo, and accepted a job with an Arab League agency.[31]

After settling in Cairo, Dr Siriyya began organizing the first Islamic

Liberation Organization cells. Friendship, and the careful observation of, and approach to, young, devout, worshippers at local mosques, represented the primary mechanisms of recruitment used.[32] The proliferation of independent (*Ahali*) mosques, free from government control, facilitated this recruitment.[33] Members of the Islamic Liberation Organization were primarily young (median age 22) students or recent graduates (professionals), from lower or lower middle-class (often rural) backgrounds. Most resided in Cairo, Alexandria and the Delta.[34] Women were not recruited.

Decision-making within the Islamic Liberation Organization was largely consensual, based on a twelve-member committee chaired by Dr Siriyya. Dr Siriyya was revered by Islamic Liberation Organization members and his advice was usually accepted during policy deliberations. The notable exception to this was the group's decision in 1974 to attack the Technical Military Academy and carry out a coup against President Sadat; although Dr Siriyya gave the scheme only a 30 per cent chance of success,[35] it was adopted and attempted on 18 April. On that date the group, despite extensive planning and practice, failed to achieve its objectives and was subsequently broken up by the Egyptian security forces.

In early 1974, the Islamic Liberation Organization became aware of the parallel activities of another underground militant Islamic organization, the Group of Muslims. Although one attempt at joining forces was made during that year, organizational and ideological differences proved insurmountable.

The ideology of the Islamic Liberation Organization was heavily influenced by the writings of Hassan al-Banna and Sayyid Qutb, as well as those of Abu al-A'la al-Mawdoudi and Ali Shariati.[36] That ideology had five core aspects:

1. That Islam provides the only proper and required path to righteous life, and that man was created to follow this path. Since the way of Islam is exclusive, other religions are godless. In this view of the world the Islamic Liberation Organization, like many other militant Islamic groups, are significantly less tolerant of Judaism and Christianity (the 'peoples of the book') than is contemporary mainstream Islam.
2. Righteousness must exist on both an individual and collective level. For the latter to occur, society must be governed by the *Shari'a*.
3. The failure of existing 'Islamic' societies (such as Egypt) to genuinely and totally adopt the *Shari'a* as their legal-political basis

has led to their weakness in the face of external enemies, notably the Christian West, Jewish Zionism and atheistic communism.

4. The establishment *ulama* are condemned as propagandists, who prop up an immoral social-political order, corrupting Islam in the process.

5. The Islamic Liberation Organization, like similar groups, see themselves engaged in *takfir* (an accusation of godlessness) against the extant political and social structure, and in a *jihad* (holy struggle) for the re-Islamification of society. Dedication to this cause is reinforced by the acceptance of the concept of martyrdom, with paradise awaiting those who fall in the struggle against godlessness.

Thus, the Islamic Liberation Organization advocated the reorganization of Egyptian society on the basis of the *Shari'a*, and the rejection of imported, non-Islamic institutions and ideas. Because the Islamic Liberation Organization differentiated between Egyptian state and society – the former godless and corrupt, the later victimized by the political system – the group advocated transformation from above. In this way it worked towards the seizure of state power, with the aim of establishing an Islamic political system through which the re-Islamification of society could take place.[37]

It was in pursuit of this revolutionary aim that, in 1974, members of the Islamic Liberation Organization adopted a two-stage plan wherein: (1) the Technical Military Academy in Cairo would be attacked, and weapons and uniforms seized; and (2) the group would move on to the headquarters of the Arab Socialist Union, where President Sadat and other Egyptian leaders would be assembled. Dr Siriyya unsuccessfully counselled against the plan, arguing that the Islamic Liberation Organization was not yet ready, and that the regime was too popular in the aftermath of the October 1973 war.[38] Nevertheless, the attack was carried out on 18 April 1974. Although the Technical Military Academy was successfully attacked, the second stage of the operation was never reached, in the face of government counter-measures.

Subsequently, many members of the Islamic Liberation Organization were captured by the Egyptian security forces. Dr Siriyya and two other Islamic Liberation Organization leaders (Karem al-Anadoli and Tallal al-Ansari) were executed, and twenty-nine others sentenced to jail terms of various durations.[39]

The Group of Muslims (Jama'at al-Musilmin)

The Group of Muslims, popularly known as al-Takfir wa al-Hijrah,[40] was founded in the early 1970s by Shukry Mustafa. Mustafa was a former member of the Muslim Brotherhood, and had been jailed for his membership in 1965. While in prison, he saw fellow Brethren either breaking down under torture or engaged in infighting. This led him to reject the political and organizational tactics of the Muslim Brotherhood (though not its ideology), and to begin the organization of his own militant Islamic group. The first members of the Group of Muslims were recruited while Mustafa was still in prison.[41]

Following his release in 1971, Mustafa set about expanding his organization. He moved to Asyut (a provincial capital in Upper Egypt), and recruited members in that area; later, he moved to Cairo. Kinship and friendship represented the primary recruitment mechanisms utilized by the Group. Those recruited were usually young (median age 24) students or recent graduates (professionals), and from middle or lower middle-class (often rural) backgrounds. The bulk of the group's members were from Upper Egypt, primarily because of Mustafa's initial residence in Asyut. Although the vast majority of the group's members were male, some women were recruited (normally through kinship ties).[42]

Decision-making within the group was autocratic in nature, with Mustafa exercising final judgement on all matters as the Amir of Jama'at al-Mu'minin ('Commander of the Faithful Group'). He was accorded considerable respect and obedience by his followers, who considered that he and the group had been ordained by God to restore Islam. The organization utilized a 'dedicated cadre' of followers – that is, the Group demanded full-time activism and total obedience, thus creating a situation wherein members were heavily dependent upon it. Deviation from duty or group doctrine could lead to expulsion, physical punishment, and even assassination.[43]

The Egyptian government estimated that, at its peak in 1977, the group boasted some 2–3,000 members and active sympathizers throughout Egypt, and financial assets of £E50,000. The group ran several small business operations, including bakeries, bookshops, candy-making, and vegetable production.[44] There was also some evidence of sympathizers in other Arab countries.[45]

The ideology of the group was, in many ways, broadly similar to that of the Islamic Liberation Organization: Ibrahim lists the writings of the Khwarjites, Ibn Taymiya, Muhammad Ibn 'Abd al-Wahhab, and Jamal al-Din al-Afghani as having influenced Mustafa, as well as those of al-Banna, Qutb, al-Mawdoudi and Shariati.[46] During his testimony before a military tribunal in 1977, Shukry Mustafa identified the group's ideology as emanating from the following principles:

- all existing societies are pagan.

- the only true Islam is the Islam of the Prophet, his companions, and the salaf [the first three generations of Muslims]. No true Islam has existed since.

- interpretation of the Koran – qiyas, ijma, and ijtihad – are rejected.

- membership in the Group of Muslims is the right path to being a good Muslim.

- not everyone who claims to be a Muslim is one. Only those who accept and live by the tenets of the Group of Muslims are good Muslims. Others are infidels.[47]

Unlike the Islamic Liberation Organization, the group made no distinction between state and society. The two were felt to be closely interrelated, and both were seen as godless and corrupt. Parallels were drawn between contemporary Egypt and the ignorance and paganism (*Jahiliyyah*) of pre-Islamic Arabia. Because of this, the group eschewed as a goal the immediate seizure of state power, viewing their task instead as a long-term one. Following the example set by the Prophet Muhammad in his flight from Mecca to Medina and his subsequent conquest of Arabia, the group sought to establish an insulated community of believers. This would then form the base from which the re-Islamification of Egyptian society could take place. The group's manifesto, *al-Khalafah*, categorized the group's mission into three stages, beginning with communications (*balagh*); followed by organi- zation, emergence (*tabaw'*), and migration; and culminating in holy war and its strategy.[48] Two sites for a community of believers were actually prepared – although never fully adopted – by the group: one in Minya Governate, the other south of Cairo.[49]

The group suffered serious arrests in May 1975, August and November 1976, and in January 1977. Members of the group subsequently claimed that it was such government suppression (more specifically, the detention without trial of several group members) that provoked it to take precipitate action against the regime in July 1977.[50] Others claim that the group's violent acts were designed to show their strength *vis-à-vis* other militant Islamic organizations.[51]

Whatever the reason, on 3 July 1977 group members kidnapped former Egyptian Minister of Waqfs (Islamic endowments) Sheikh Muhammad al-Dahabi, a noted Islamic scholar and strong opponent of religious extremism. A ransom of £E200,000, the release of sixty prisoners, and an aircraft were demanded for al-Dahabi's release. The demands were not met, and three days later Sheikh al-Dahabi's body was found in a deserted apartment in al-Haram district. A series of bombings were carried out over the next few days by the group. Intensive action by the Egyptian security forces, however, soon led to the arrest of Mustafa and 400 other members. Of these, 198 were tried in court, with 36 eventually being found guilty. Five group leaders, including Shukry Mustafa, were ultimately executed for their activities.[52]

At the time, the arrests and Mustafa's execution were widely thought to have put an end to the group. By the 1980s, however, it was clear that this was not the case. Certainly, the loss of Mustafa was a heavy blow to an organization so firmly structured around his person and personality: indeed, his presence had been such that many group members refused at first to believe he was dead. When it became clear that he was, many drifted away from the group and either joined other militant Islamic organizations, or left the Islamic movement altogether. Still others emigrated to Yemen, where they hoped to find more suitable conditions for the establishment of an Islamic society.[53]

Nevertheless, a minority of dedicated group members did seek to rebuild the shattered organization. A new governing structure was set up outside Egypt under the leadership of Muhammad Amin 'Abd-al-Fattah. A nine-member advisory council was created in Egypt to implement the instructions of this external leadership. The membership of the reconstituted group is estimated at roughly 150 people in Egypt, and a somewhat larger number outside the country. It is also reported that the group aligns its policy with that of the Islamic Liberation Party.[54]

Al-Jihad (Holy Struggle)

The militant Islamic organization known as al-Jihad has a complex and not fully understood organizational history. Indeed, al-Jihad barely existed as a formal organizational entity; instead it usually took the form of loosely co-ordinated sub-groups.[55] For the purposes of analysis, however, Jihad-A, Jihad-B, Jihad-C, etc. will be used to refer to the organization at various stages in its evolution. It was Jihad-B which was responsible for the group's most spectacular exploit, the assassination of President Anwar al-Sadat in October 1981.

Although al-Jihad drew its members from the Muslim Brotherhood, the university-based Islamic Jama'at, and a variety of other sources,[56] its genealogy can be traced back to the Islamic Liberation Organization of Dr Salih Siriyya. During the suppression of the Islamic Liberation Organization by the government in 1974, two Islamic Liberation Organization members (Hasan al-Halawi and Salim al-Rahhal)[57] escaped arrest. They subsequently began setting up a new militant Islamic organization (Jihad-A), primarily in Alexandria. In August 1977 this organization was uncovered and broken up by the authorities, with some eighty members (including al-Halawi) being arrested.[58]

With the suppression of Jihad-A's top leadership, a new individual assumed a key role in the organization. Muhammad 'Abd-al-Salam Faraj, a former member of Jihad-A, set about reorganizing al-Jihad. Al-Faraj wrote a pamphlet entitled *al-Farida al-Ghai'ba* ('The Neglected Imperative'), which the authorities later described as Jihad-B's constitution.

Faraj, who assumed the role of Jihad-B's chief ideologue, was joined in the leadership by a colonel in Egyptian military intelligence, Abbud al-Zumur, who assumed charge of the organization's military planning and training; and Karem Zuhdi, who was in charge of organization and recruitment in Upper Egypt. In 1980 a consultative council (Majlis al-Shura) was established for Jihad-B, with functional subcommittees being set up to co-ordinate and oversee military training, fundraising, and recruitment. Chairmanship of the council was offered to Sheikh Omar Abd al-Rahman, a 43-year-old blind religious instructor at al-Azhar's Asyut branch.[59] Sheikh al-Rahman issued religious opinions legitimizing Jihad-B activities. In 1981 a *fatwa* (edict) issued by him was interpreted by the group as justifying theft from Egyptian Copts.[60]

Jihad-B's recruitment was primarily carried out through kinship and friendship ties, and through careful contacts made with devout young worshippers at local mosques. An analysis by Hamied Ansari of 280 Jihad-B members arrested by the government found that most resided in Upper Egypt (65 per cent) or Greater Cairo (26 per cent). Most were young (70 per cent aged 21–30) and from lower middle-class backgrounds. Students represented the largest group (43.9 per cent), followed by workers (14.6 per cent), professionals (12.5 per cent) and the unemployed (10.7 per cent).[61]

Jihad-B was financed by contributions, and by the robbery of Copt-owned jewellery stores. Some funds may also have been provided by al-Jihad members outside Egypt. The group's total assets were valued at £E17,000.[62]

Jihad-B suffered considerable organizational damage during Sadat's September 1981 clampdown against domestic opposition. This had the effect of exacerbating the militancy of Jihad-B members still at large, culminating in the assassination of al-Sadat on October 6.[63] In the aftermath of the assassination, much of Jihad-B was broken up by the Egyptian security forces. Hundreds were arrested, and five Jihad-B members (including Al-Faraj) were executed for their part in the plot. In 1984, following three years of trial, 190 members of Jihad-B were acquitted and released, among them the *mufti*, Sheikh Omar Abd al-Rahman. Seventeen others were imprisoned for life, including Karem Zuhdi and Abbud al-Zumur.[64]

Following the suppression of Jihad-B in late 1981, a number of attempts to reorganize and reconstruct the group were made. One of these (identified here as 'Jihad-C') was broken up by the authorities in September 1982, with most of the group's leadership being arrested. The total membership of Jihad-C prior to its suppression was estimated at 200, and the group was said to have acquired twelve weapons and materials for several bombs.[65]

Jihad-C successfully managed to contact al-Jihad members in prison, and received three smuggled letters from Abbud al-Zumur advising on the group's operations. Jihad-C is also reported to have attempted to contact the Iranian government through Abbud al-Zumur's younger brother, Muhammad 'Abd-al-Salam al-Zumur.[66] Like Jihad-B, Jihad-C sought to legitimize its underground activities by consulting a militant religious figure, in this case Sheikh Hafiz Salamah. Sheikh Salamah was a former member of the Muslim Brotherhood, a current leader in the Islamic Jama'at, and chairman of Suez's Islamic Guidance Society.[67] Accounts of the one meeting held between Sheikh Salamah and the leaders of Jihad-C vary: the former claims to have counselled against militant activities, while some of the latter claim that Sheikh Salamah rejected only certain types of action (an attempt to rescue jailed al-Jihad members), while advocating others (a programme of assassinations).[68]

The ideology of al-Jihad was set forward by Muhammad al-Faraj in *al-Faridha al-Ghai'ba*. The pamphlet describes 'the establishment of the Islamic state and the restoration of the Khalafah' as 'the duty of every Muslim'.[69] This is the neglected imperative to which Jihad-B is dedicated

Maintaining that the domain of Islam has been transformed into the domain of infidelity because 'the rulers of this age have abandoned the faith and are the servants of imperialism,'[70] Al-Faraj argues that a true Muslim's duty is to struggle for the establishment of the Islamic state:[71] 'Jihad is an imperative for every Muslim'.[72] Propagation of the Islamic state is not sufficient.[73] 'The Muslim must prepare himself to struggle for the sake of God.'[74] The Islamic state, once established, will be indestructible because it is God's will. 'In addition, Islamic laws are neither deficient nor feeble and will subjugate every corrupt person on this earth who goes against God's will.... Furthermore, God's laws are all just and will be welcomed by everyone, including those who do not know Islam.'[75] The objective of al-Jihad was thus the establishment of an Islamic state and society, i.e. one based on the adoption of, and adherence to, the *Shari'a* as the basis of political and social life. All those who opposed the ordering of human existence on that basis were considered by al-Jihad to be unbelievers to be struggled against. The list of these enemies thus included those of other religions (including Ahl al-Kitab, the Jewish and Christian 'people of the book'), atheists, secularists, and Muslims who had accommodated to contemporary Egyptian society (including the religious establishment).[76]

Al-Jihad, like its Islamic Liberation Organization predecessor, drew a distinction between state and society, and aimed at the seizure of state power: 'we proceed from the top to the bottom because we believe that a good ruler can create everything in society'.[77] However, whereas the Islamic Liberation Organization eschewed popular revolt as a route to such power (viewing such revolts as 'communistic')[78], al-Jihad had appeared to have accepted the strategy as a legitimate one – doubtless as a result of the revolution in Iran. Nevertheless, al-Jihad leaders still maintained that mass support was not necessary or perhaps not even achievable: not only was mass propaganda difficult to disseminate successfully in a society controlled by unbelievers but, in addition, the righteousness of the militants' cause guaranteed them victory.[79]

With regard to militant activities, it is clear that the early form of the group (al-Jihad-A) engaged primarily in recruitment and organization. Jihad-A did, however, manage to acquire weapons and explosives. It was in search of such arms that Jihad-A members shot and killed an Egyptian guard outside the Cypriot Consulate in Alexandria in July 1977.[80]

Jihad-B engaged in a number of paramilitary activities. Thefts from police and army weapons stores were undertaken. Jihad-B members were active in violent student demonstrations in Asyut in 1980.[81] The group played a significant role in sectarian conflict with Egypt's Coptic community, first in Upper Egypt and later throughout the country. Group members instigated sectarian clashes, robbed Christian jewellery stores, attacked Coptic churches, bombed a Coptic wedding, and warned that Egypt's Copts were armed and a threat to Islam. Jihad-B was active in the sectarian fighting which erupted in Cairo's Zawiya al-Hamra district in June 1981.[82]

Jihad-B's most important action, however, was the assassination of Egyptian President Anwar al-Sadat, by four al-Jihad sympathizers on 6 October 1981. Two days after Sadat's assassination, fifty Jihad-B members attacked security forces in Asyut. In the fighting which followed, 118 persons (including 54 members of the security forces) died and over 200 were wounded.[83] Many other, smaller clashes took place as the security forces sought out and arrested Jihad-B members.

Jihad-C only undertook activities of an organizational nature. The group did, however, consider three plans whereby it would either: (1) attempt to rescue imprisoned Jihad members in conjunction with an airline hijacking at Cairo airport; or (2) engage in a series of attacks and assassinations of government targets; or (3) attempt a combination of the two plans whereby the group would also seize arms under cover of a local riot or uprising.[84]

The Islamic militants and the 'legal' Islamic movements

In all three cases discussed above, the underground militants have enjoyed an ambivalent relationship with quasi-legal Islamic movements in Egypt such as the university-based Islamic Jama'at and the Muslim Brotherhood. In the latter case, the Brotherhood, anxious to retain some vestiges of legality and viewing itself in a 'missionary' rather than a 'revolutionary' role, has condemned many of the more violent activities of Egypt's Islamic militants. At the same time, it has attributed the growth of Islamic militancy in Egypt to government repression (particularly under Nasser) and the government's deviation from Islam. Significantly, the Muslim Brotherhood has refused to accept the militants' interpretation of *al-takfir* and their concomitant violent opposition to the Islamic establishment, arguing instead that all who pronounce the *Shahada* (the Muslim declaration of faith in God and the Prophethood of Muhammad should be considered Muslims, regardless of their sins.[85] This, together with the gradualist tactics and reformist approach of the contemporary Brotherhood, have often drawn scorn from many of Egypt's Islamic militants.

Nevertheless, it is also important to recognize that many significant and varied ties exist between the underground Islamic militants on the one hand, and the quasi-legal Muslim Brotherhood and Islamic Jama'at on the other. While their prescriptions may differ considerably, all of these groups advance a broadly similar analysis and critique of Egyptian government and society. Furthermore, the Muslim Brotherhood and Islamic Jama'at have represented a lucrative recruiting and training ground for the militant groups. The university-based Islamic Jama'at, for example, has provided a natural cover for the propaganda and recruitment activities of Egypt's young (often student) militant Islamic activists. Many Islamic Jama'at members or leaders have been or are members of underground organizations, or have family or personal links with such groups. Similarly, former Muslim Brethren have often provided leadership (e.g. Shukry Mustafa) or advice (e.g. Sheikh Salamah, who was also an Islamic Jama'at leader) to the militants. There is also some evidence that the government crackdown against opposition groups immediately before and after Sadat's assassination served to reinforce the ties between quasi-legal and underground Islamic forces in Egypt. According to Ibrahim, evidence of such a reconciliation was provided by the participation of militant leaders in the 1983 funeral of prominent Muslim Brethren member Salih 'Ashmawi.[86]

NOTES

1. For example, 'New Worry Over Spread of Iran's Revolution', *US News & World Report*, 7 June 1982, pp. 51–2.
2. See Tareq Y. Ismael, *The Arab Left*, Syracuse, Syracuse University Press, 1976.
3. Although *al-I'tisam* was officially published by the Shari'a Society (rather than the Muslim Brotherhood) and was initially concerned with theological matters, it gradually adopted a more political stance – mirroring *al-Da'wa*'s position and using many of the same writers.
   Saad Eddin Ibrahim, 'An Islamic Alternative in Egypt: The Muslim Brotherhood and Sadat', *Arab Studies Quarterly* IV/1–2, 1982, p. 181.
4. Hasan Hanafi, 'al-Din wa al-Tanmujah fi Misr' in Saad Eddin Ibrahim (ed.), *Misr fi Ruba' Qirn, 1952–1977*, Beirut, Mahad al-Inm'a al-'Arabi, 1981, pp. 275–9.
5. By the late 1970s, *al-Da'wa* and *al-I'tisam* boasted circulations of roughly 100,000 each.
   Ibrahim, 'The Muslim Brotherhood and Sadat', op. cit., p. 81.
6. Muhammad Heikal, *Autumn of Fury*, London, Andre Deutsch, 1983, p. 133.
7. See Roger Owen, 'Sadat's Legacy, Mubarak's Dilemma', *Merip Reports*, September 1983, pp. 12–18.

124   *Modern Activism*

8. Heikal, op. cit., pp. 84–9.
   For an American perspective on the contrast between Nasser and Sadat in general, and of *infitah* in particular, see John Waterbury, *The Egypt of Nasser and Sadat: the Political Economy of Two Regimes*, Princeton, Princeton University Press, 1983.
9. Ali E. Hillal Dessouki, 'The Primacy of Economics: The Foreign Policy of Egypt' in Baghat Korany and Ali E. Hillal Dessouki (eds), *The Foreign Policy of Arab States*, Boulder, Co., Westview Press, 1984, pp. 125–6.
10. Edward Mortimer, *Faith and Power: the Politics of Islam*, London, Faber, 1982, p. 291.
11. Ali E. Hillal Dessouki, 'The Shift in Egypt's Migration Policy: 1952–1979', *Middle Eastern Studies*, 18, 1, January 1982.
12. Heikal, *Autumn of Fury*, p. 185.
13. *Al-Ahram al-Iqtisadi*, Cairo, 25 January 1982.
14. Saad Eddin Ibrahim, 'Anatomy of Egypt's Militant Islamic Groups', *International Journal of Middle East Studies* XII/4, December 1980, p. 434.
15. Sayyid Qutb, *Milestones*, International Islamic Federation of Student Organizations, 1978.
16. Ibid., p. 15.
17. Ibid,, p. 32.
18. Ibid., p. 15.
19. Ibid., pp. 11, 236–7.
20. Ibid., pp. 164–6.
21. Ibid., p. 220. In support of this view Qutb cites Sura IV:78:
    'Those who believe fight in the cause of God, and those who disbelieve fight in the cause of rebellion. Then fight the allies of Satan; indeed, Satan's strategy is weak.'
22. Ibid., p. 220. 'This is My straight path. Then follow it, and do not follow other ways which will scatter you from His path' (Sura VI:153).
23. Ibid., p. 221. 'We have set thee on a way ordained [by God]; then follow it, and do not follow the desires of those who have no knowledge' (Sura XXXXV:18).
24. Ibid., pp. 243–4.
25. Ibid., pp. 211–12.
26. Ibid., p. 245.
27. Ibid., pp. 138–9.
28. Ibid., p. 17.
29. This group is also known as the 'Technical Military Academy group' (Jam'at al-Fanniyya al-Askariyya), a name given to them by the Arab media following the group's attack on Cairo's Technical Military Academy in April 1974.
30. On the Islamic Liberation Party, see Chapter 6.
31. Ibrahim, 'Anatomy of Egypt's Militant Islamic Groups', op. cit., pp. 435–6.
32. Ibid., p. 438.
33. An estimated 20,000 *Ahali* mosques may have existed in Egypt in 1970, growing to over 40,000 by 1980. In contrast, only 6,000 mosques (1980) were controlled by the Egyptian Ministry of Waqfs (Islamic endowments). See Hamied N. Ansari, 'The Islamic Militants in Egyptian Politics',

International Journal of Middle East Studies XVI/1, March 1984, pp. 125–6.
34. Ibrahim, op. cit., pp. 438–9.
35. Ibid., p. 437.
36. Ibid., pp. 435–6.
37. Ibid., pp. 429–35, 441.
38. Ibid., p. 437.
39. *Arab Report and Record*, 16–31 May 1975, p. 306.
40. Al-Takfir wa al-Hijrah ('Excommunication and Holy Flight') is a name assigned to the group by the Egyptian media and authorities. The title refers to the organization's accusation of godlessness (*al-Takfir*) against Egyptian society, and its call for a separation from that society akin to the Prophet's flight from Mecca (*al-Hijrah*).
41. Ibrahim, op. cit., p. 436.
42. Ibid., pp. 437–9.
43. Ibid., pp. 438–41. In fact, it was the Muslim Group's punishment of deviant members in 1976–7 that alerted the Egyptian autorities to its activities. See also 'Abd al-Rahman Abut al-Khayr, *Dhikriyat ma' Jama'at al-Muslimun*, Kuwait, Dar al-Buhuth al-'Ilmiyah, 1980, pp. 71, 82–3. *Al-Akhbar*, Cairo, 24 November 1976.
44. *Arab Report and Record*, 1 15 July 1977, pp. 531–2.
45. Following the arrest of Group members in July 1977, a threat to bomb the Egyptian Embassy was reported in Kuwait. *Arab Report and Record*, 16–31 July 1977, p. 587.
46. Ibrahim, op. cit., p. 435.
47 *Al-Ahram*, Cairo, 21 October 1979; *Al-Mussawar*, Cairo, No. 3009, 11 June 1982.
48. Al-Khayr, *Dhikriyat ma' Jama'at al-Muslimun*, p. 81.
49. Ibrahim, op. cit., p. 452.
50. Ibid., pp. 442–3.
51. *Al-Majallah*, London, 25 May 1984, pp. 8–10.
52. *Arab Report and Record*, 1–15 July 1977, pp. 531–2. *Al-Majallah*, London, 25 May 1984, pp. 8–10.
53. *Al-Majallah*, op. cit.
54. Ibid.
55. Ansari, op. cit., pp. 125–6.
56. In Asyut; a leading member of al-Jihad was related by marriage to Shukry Mustafa.
57. Al-Rahhal was Palestinian by birth. *Al-Mussawar*, Cairo, 24 September 1982, pp. 4–9.
58. Ibid. *Arab Report and Record*, 16–31 August 1977, pp. 673–4.
59. Ansari, op. cit., p. 126.
60. Hamied N. Ansari, 'Sectarian Conflict in Egypt and the Political Expediency of Religion', *Middle East Journal*, XXXVIII/3, Summer 1984, p. 415.
61. Ansari, 'Islamic Militants in Egyptian Politics', pp. 131–4.
62. Ibid., pp. 126–7.
63. Ibid., pp. 128, 130.
64. *Asharq al-Ausat*, London, 1 October 1984.

65. *Al-Mussawar*, Cairo, 24 September 1982, pp. 4–9.
66. Ibid.
67. *Al-Mussawar*, Cairo, 11 September 1981, pp. 10, 11, 65.
68. *Al-Mussawar*, Cairo, 24 September 1982, pp. 4–9.
69. *Al-Faridha al-Ghai'ba*, p. 7. This pamphlet has been reprinted in many places, and has been widely circulated throughout the world among Muslim communities. The pamphlet bears no publication data. It is generally prefaced by a quotation from Sayyid Qutb.
70. Ibid., p. 9.
71. Ibid., pp. 14–15.
72. Ibid., p. 21.
73. Ibid., p. 15.
74. Ibid., p. 22.
75. Ibid., p. 21.
76. Ansari, op. cit., pp. 136–8.
77. Karem Zudhi, quoted in ibid., p. 414.
78. Ibrahim, op. cit., p. 443.
79. Ansari, op. cit., p. 127.
80. *Arab Report and Record*, 16–31 August 1977, p. 674.
81. Ansari, op. cit., p. 127.
82. Ansari, 'Sectarian Conflict in Egypt', op. cit., pp. 408–15.
83. *The Times*, London, 12 October 1981, p. 4.
84. *Al-Mussawar*, Cairo, 24 September 1982, pp. 4–9.
85. Ansari, 'Islamic Militants in Egyptian Politics', op. cit., p. 140.
    Al-Watan al-Arabi, London, No. 240, 24 September 1981, pp. 38–41.
86. *Al-Majallah*, London, 3–9 March 1984, pp. 33–4.

6 Islamic Politics Today

Contemporary Islamic political activism is an expression of the fundamental unity of spiritual and temporal affairs that is the foundation of the Islamic belief system. This assumption of unity has been manifested throughout Islamic history in the socio-cultural patterns of Islam as a way of life – signifying not only the unity of spiritual beliefs across diverse peoples and times but also a pervasive orientation to the temporal world that constitutes a continuous, if ambiguous, cultural pattern across time and place in Islamic history. Sadiq Jalal al-Azm, an eminent secular scholar of Arab society, summarized this cultural influence as:

> . . . a tremendous force which enters into the depth of our lives and influences the essence of the intellectual, social and psychological structures. It represents guidelines as to the ways of thinking and reacting towards the world, and is an inseparable aspect of social behaviour. It is looked upon as a group of beliefs, rituals and institutions which surround the masses irrespective of their social, cultural or class status in every comprehensive way.[1]

The development and evolution of Islamic political thought is a product of the assumption of spiritual and temporal unity. In its normative orientation, it is a search for that unity through the political sphere; and in its analytic orientation, a search for understanding of the failure of political institutions to realize that unity. Contemporary Islamic political activism emanates directly from this dialectic. The two interrelated themes running through Islamic political thought – political legitimacy and political accountability – are the themes of contemporary Islamic political activism. These themes are manifested on two levels: in the efforts of various regimes to legitimate their rule officially through Islam; and in the efforts of various popular activist groups to challenge the legitimacy of existing regimes on the grounds of accountability to Islamic codes.

Official legitimation

The traditional role of Islam in the legitimation of government was established in Part I. Even among the secularized states of the modern era, official Islamic legitimation has been viewed as a cultural imperative and used as a political tool. But with the emergence of an Islamic activist movement, it has become a political imperative. The cases examined in Part II reflect the nature of this political imperative. Here we overview Libya and the Sudan as further examples of revolutionary legitimation on the one hand and status quo legitimation on the other. In addition, the use of Islam as a political tool is most clearly exemplified in the foreign policy sphere and is reviewed in terms of the development of international Islamic organizations.

Libya

In the immediate aftermath of the 1969 revolution which toppled King Idris, the new Revolutionary Command Council which ruled Libya instituted a number of Islamic measures. The sale and consumption of alcohol was forbidden, nightclubs were closed down, and a decree calling for the precedence of the Hijra calendar over the Gregorian calendar on official documents was issued. In October 1969, an Egyptian jurist was invited to investigate how the *Shari'a* might replace extant Libyan laws. Following his report in 1970, the Revolutionary Command Council issued a decree in October 1972 that, in future, the compatibility of new laws with the *Shari'a* had to be taken into consideration when they were formulated. Furthermore, committees were set up to assess the compatibility of existing laws with the *Shari'a*, and Islamic punishment codes were introduced.

Islamic symbolism and concern with Islamic issues continues to be a prominent feature of the regime of Colonel Muammar al-Qadhdafi into the 1980s. Nevertheless, two aspects of such Islam need to be noted. The first is its idiosyncratic nature: al-Qaddafi has stressed a (personal) view of Islam which departs from the norm in its emphasis on the importance of *ijtihad*, de-emphasis of the role of the Sunna, and attacks on the traditionalism and rigidity of the religious establishment and their interference in the private relationship between man and God. This stance, and Qadhdafi's introduction of unorthodox religious reforms (such as his unilateral amendment of the Hijra calendar) have led to hostile relations between his government and many traditional *ulama*.

The second significant feature of Qadaffi's Islam is its function as a legitimator of the regime. In his *al-Kitab al-Akhdar* (Green Book), for example, Qadhdafi sets forth in his 'Third Universal Theory', upon which the social, political and economic structure of the Libyan revolution is to be based. Significantly, religion's role within that theory is primarily confined to the strengthening of national unity.[2] Qadhdafi has criticized Libyan imams for mixing politics and religion in their Friday sermons, stating that 'sermons on Fridays must deal with those matters which man has come to the mosque to seek, which are prayer and God's remembrance only'.[3] In addition to his conflict with the traditional religious establishment, Qadhdafi has suppressed the Muslim Brotherhood and similar Islamic organizations, reportedly stating that he 'does not believe that the Muslim Brothers represent a Muslim philosophy in the true sense of the word . . . they are against socialism, against Arab unity, against Arab nationalism: so far as they preach Islamic unity they cannot but oppose Arab unity . . . both they and the Islamic Liberation Party are mere agents of the West.'[4]

This subordination of Islam to Qadhdafi's personal views and regime goals has also occurred in the foreign policy sphere. While Libya has supported some Muslim minorities against non-Muslim governments (e.g. in the Philippines), it has also done the reverse (e.g. Sudan). Moreover, it enjoys better relations with some secular leftist forces in the Islamic world (e.g. the Popular Front for the Liberation of Palestine and the Arab communist parties) than it does with many revolutionary Islamic organizations (e.g. the Lebanese Shiah militia Amal, many of whose members hold Qadhdafi responsible for the disappearance of Lebanese Shiah leader Imam Musa Sadr).

Sudan

One example of state sponsorship of Islamic ideology can be found in the Sudan. While most observers accept Sudanese President Ja'far Muhammad Numayri's personal commitment to Islam as deep and genuine (albeit relatively recently acquired), his government's use of Islamic symbols and rationale for the legitimation of foreign and domestic policy, its co-optation of some domestic Islamic forces within the regime, and its suppression of other such forces – all these represent characteristic elements of what might be called 'official Islam'. Because of this, examination of the Sudanese case provides valuable insight into the growth, substance and development of this phenomenon.

The May 1969 revolution, which first brought Numayri to power as

President of the Revolutionary Command Council, was far from Islamic in inspiration. Instead, it drew its support from an alliance of leftists and army officers who wished to forestall any return to power by Sadiq al-Mahdi, the (Islamic modernist) leader of the Umma Party. Reflecting this, the first revolutionary cabinet was decidedly secular-socialist in political orientation. Numayri, in fact, was considered to be very sympathetic to the Communist Party and its strongest supporter among the Free Officers in the Revolutionary Command Council.[5]

By 1971, however, a major split had developed within the Revolutionary Command Council over the implementation of socialism and Sudanese participation in the proposed Arab Federation. The Communist Party of Sudan split with Numayri. In July 1971, an adventurous army officer sympathetic to the Communist Party, though not a member, attempted an unsuccessful coup. In its aftermath, Numayri launched a witchhunt against Communists, executing the party's leadership and many members.

It was after the July coup that Numayri began to clothe his administration in Islamic garb. Recognizing the power and inherent anti-communism of Islamic appeals, Numayri purged his cabinet of leftists and appointed a number of individuals from Sufi backgrounds to senior governmental positions. The President's own personal piety was also emphasized.[6] Numayri then began to advocate the explicit reordering of Sudanese government along Islamic lines. The 1973 Constitution, for example, recognized Islamic law and custom as 'the main sources of legislation'. The following January, Numayri told the Sudanese Socialist Union that 'the role of religion should not be thought of as confined to the level of individuals and the sphere of ethics only, for religion is the cornerstone and basis of all social and political institutions in society as a whole.[7] In April 1977 a Committee for the Revision of Sudanese Law was formed to bring the Sudanese legal system into accordance with Islamic principles.

Such measures were accompanied by a process of 'National Reconciliation' whereby Numayri co-opted those political forces which supported his Islamic reforms into the regime, while suppressing all other groups. The co-operative wing of the Muslim Brotherhood led by Hasan al-Turabi was the most prominent group to accept access to political power in exchange for integration into Sudan's only recognized political party, the Sudanese Socialist Union.[8] Sadiq al-Mahdi, while remaining outside the regime, maintained a *de facto* truce with the government after 1977.

In 1980 Numayri published a book in which he articulated his belief that Islam represented the ideal model of social and political organization.[9] This marked an intensification of the pace of Islamic reform in the Sudan, culminating in Numayri's declaration of Islamic law in September 1983. This declaration was accompanied by the pardoning of 13,000 criminals and the destruction of Khartoum's liquor supply. Nine months later, Numayri proposed draft constitutional amendments designed to make the Democratic Republic of Sudan a 'sovereign united Islamic republic'.[10]

Numayri's espousal of official Islam, though popular, was not without its problems. While it satisfied some elements of the Muslim Brotherhood, Numayri found himself in competition with them as each sought to outbid the other in their commitment to Islamification. Moreover, Numayri found himself under criticism from Sadiq al-Mahdi for the harshness and rigidity of the implementation of Islamic law. Finally, the regime's Islamic measures were unpopular with the Christian and animist South, and exacerbated the widespread seccessionist sentiment already found there. Numayri responded to such challenges by 'promoting' al-Turabi from Public Prosecutor to the more senior, but less powerful, position of Presidential Advisor, and by arresting Sidiq in October 1983.[11] In April 1984 a state of emergency was declared in the country.

International Islamic organizations

The first modern calls for the formation of an international Islamic organization go back roughly one hundred years, to the debate over resisting the expansion of European influence through the formation of an Islamic league. Thereafter, what Islamic unity remained was shattered by World War I, whose aftermath saw most of the Muslim countries under European control. The final blow came in 1924 with Attaturk's abolition of the Islamic *Khalafah* and the secularization of Turkey.

As a result of European domination, nationalism, rather than Islamic unity, became the dominant political force in Muslim countries, with talk about Islamic unity being largely confined to literature and inter-Arab treaties. One exception to this was the Islamic Congress which took place in Cairo in 1926. This Congress, which was convened at the request of King Abd al-Aziz al-Saud, inconclusively discussed the vacant Khalifate, a title for which several Muslim leaders (including Shariff Hussain of Hijaz and King Fuad I of Egypt) were competing. Subsequent Congresses were held in Mecca in 1926 (to discuss religious issues), and in Jerusalem in 1931 (to promote pan-Islamic support for the struggle against Britain and the Zionist movement in Palestine).

The end of World War II saw many of the Islamic countries gain their independence, and the call arose for Islamic unity among the new states. Pakistan played a particularly significant role in this, hosting conferences – primarily on economic issues – in February 1949, November 1949 and May 1952. Over the next decades a number of Islamic organizations emerged:

1. World Islamic Congress: first convened in 1926, and later in Jerusalem 1931, Karachi 1949 and 1951, Baghdad in 1962 and Mogadishu in 1964.

2. The General Islamic Congress: formed in 1955 under the auspices of the Egyptian government with Anwar Sadat as its General Secretary. This conference established many Islamic centres in foreign countries, the most prominent of which was in Mogadishu. It convened the first congress of Islamic *ulama* in Cairo in 1966.

3. The Islamic Conference Seminar: formed in Jerusalem in 1953, and which convened later in Damascus 1956, and Jerusalem 1960 and 1961.

4. The Muslim World League: formed by a decision in the Islamic Conference which convened in Mecca in 1962. The League attempted to found a system of Islamic banking and establish a broadcasting station (Voice of Islam) directed at countries in Asia, Africa and Europe. It also established a newspaper, *Akhbar al-'Alam al-Islami*.

5. The World Islamic Federation: established in Paris in order to spread knowledge of Islam, and to organize the Muslim communities.

6. The Afro-Asian Islamic Organization: formed in 1965.

7. The International Islamic Organization: formed in 1970 during the first meeting of the Islamic Afro-Asian organizations in Bandung.

Most of these organizations were unable to achieve consensus among the Islamic countries, and in many cases they served as arenas of dispute among differing governments. However, the 1967 war and the arson attack on the al-Aqsa Mosque in occupied Jerusalem on 21 August 1969 led to an Islamic conference of the leaders of twenty-seven Islamic states in Rabat (Morocco) during the period 22–27 September 1969. The Islamic Conference discussed the developments in the Middle East conflict and the policies that the Islamic countries should pursue in order to preserve the holy Islamic shrines.

It also declared that 'their governments shall consult together with a view to promoting among themselves close co-operation and mutual assistance in the economic, scientific, cultural and spiritual fields, inspired by the immortal teachings of Islam',[12] and called for the formation of an Islamic Conference Organization. The Foreign Ministers of the Islamic Conference held their first annual meeting in Jeddah the following year, 23–25 March 1970. At their third meeting, in February–March 1972, thirty Foreign Ministers formally endorsed a Charter for the Islamic Conference Organization.[13]

The 1972 Charter states that the Islamic Conference consists of the Conference of Kings and Heads of State and Government (since 1981, to meet every three years); the Conference of Foreign Ministers (to meet annually); and a General Secretariat (see Fig. 2). The latter,

ORGANIZATION OF THE ISLAMIC CONFERENCE

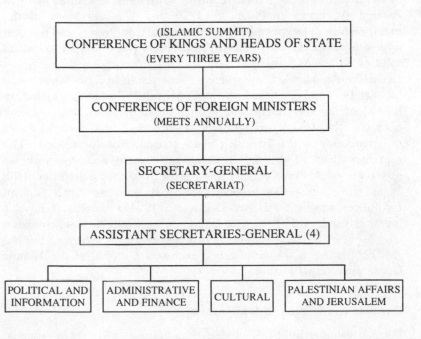

headed by a General Secretary with a three-year term, is divided into four departments – Political and Information, Administrative and Finance, Cultural, and Palestinian Affairs and Jerusalem – each headed by an Assistant Secretary-General. Over a dozen agencies operate under the aegis of the Islamic Conference Organization,[14] as well as numerous cultural and research centres.

By 1984 there had been four summit meetings of the Kings and Heads of State and Government of the Islamic Conference Organization. The second such meeting, convened in Lahore during 22 to 24 February 1974, was attended by thirty-five states. The Summit emphasized the directives of the first conference regarding the Palestinian problem and Jerusalem, and preceded the Rabat Summit Conference of the Arab League in recognizing the PLO as the sole legitimate representative of the Palestinian people. The Summit also discussed issues regarding the new international economic order.

The Third Islamic Conference was convened in Taif, Saudi Arabia during 25 to 28 January 1981. This Summit, which was held in the aftermath of the Egyptian-Israeli peace treaty, Israel's annexation and declaration of Jerusalem as its eternal indivisible capital, and the Soviet invasion of Afghanistan, affirmed previous decisions made at Foreign Minister's meetings in 1979 and 1980 to suspend the memberships of Egypt and Afghanistan. The Conference also restated its position regarding the Palestinian problem and called for a political solution to the Afghani war.

The Fourth Islamic Conference was convened in Casablanca on 16 January 1984 and discussed a number of Middle East issues, including Jerusalem, the Palestinians, the Reagan peace initiative, the Lebanese problem, the US–Israeli strategic accord and the declaration of independence by the Turkish (Islamic) community on Cyprus. The representatives of this latter community were accepted only as observers, while Benin was accepted as the forty-fourth member of the organization. The Conference supported the Fez Arab summit resolution on the Arab–Israeli dispute. It also reinstated Egypt's membership in the Islamic Conference Organization, thus provoking a walk-out by Syria, Libya and South Yemen. Habib Chatti of Tunisia was confirmed as the continuing Secretary General of the Islamic Conference Organization.

Popular challenges to legitimacy

Popular Islamic political activism has become a dynamic force in

Middle East politics. The ability of the movement to mobilize the masses and effect revolution was clearly demonstrated in Iran and manifested in Egypt. Here we survey the movement in Jordan, Syria and North Africa to overview its scope and strength.

Jordan

Both Jordan and the occupied West Bank show clear evidence of Islamic political activism. In the former case, the Muslim Brotherhood is said to have a sizeable Jordanian following, while in the latter case Islamic activism has emerged as a significant challenge to the dominance of nationalist forces.[15] Nevertheless, Jordan's major contribution to popular Islam has been in the form of an international Islamic organization, the Islamic Liberation Party.

The Islamic Liberation Party (Hizb al-Tahrir al-Islami) is a small organization, albeit one with cells in a number of countries. Very little is known about the group. It was founded in Jordan in 1948 by Shaykh Taqiyy al-Din al-Nabahani, an al-Azhar-educated 'alim who taught at the College of Science in Amman. The group is variously described as an offshoot of the Muslim Brotherhood, and as a rival organization which found its expansion into Egypt blocked, until the 1970s, by the Muslim Brotherhood's greater attractiveness to potential Islamic Liberation Party recruits. Regardless of its origins (and the latter appears more accurate), the modern Islamic Liberation Party is clearly an independent and autonomous organization. It is said to have branches in a number of Islamic countries (the largest being in Syria), as well as in Europe (particularly Austria and West Germany). The party publishes pamphlets setting forth its ideas, and organizes study groups. It also recruits new members, particularly among young transient workers from Islamic countries in Europe. With the death of Shaykh al-Nabahani, leadership of the Islamic Liberation Party is reported to have passed to his son.

In Syria, the Islamic Liberation Party is among those Islamic groups fighting the government of Hafez al-Asad. On the occupied West Bank, Israeli forces have arrested a number of Islamic Liberation Party members. In January 1984, the Tunisian authorities also arrested Islamic Liberation Party members. In Egypt, where the party's literature is commonly uncovered by police raids, the organization is believed to have had an intermittent presence since 1955. The extent of the Islamic Liberation Party's involvement with Dr Saliah Siriyya's Islamic Liberation Organization and other militant Islamic groups is, however, unknown (although the reconstituted Group of Muslims is said to co-ordinate policy with it). Furthermore, it is known that at least one attempt to establish Islamic Liberation Party cells in Egypt was made by 'Ala' al-Zanati in the late 1970s. Zanati was recruited by the Islamic Liberation Party while working in Austria. He subsequently returned to Egypt, organizing an underground Islamic Liberation Party structure while attending the College of Engineering at Cairo University. Those recruited were primarily students and young professionals. In mid-1983, al-Zanati's organizational efforts came to an end when he and thirty other members of the group were arrested by the Egyptian security forces.

The Islamic Liberation Party argues that all present-day states are in a state of godlessness, and that a world-wide Islamic state must be created to rectify this. Such a state would be based on the *Shari'a* and ruled by a Khalife. Like the Islamic Liberation Organization, the Islamic Liberation Party draws a distinction between state and society: the state and/or the people of a country may be godless, depending on their adherence to the *Shari'a*.

According to al-Zanati, the Islamic Liberation Party believes that three stages must be followed in establishing the Islamic state. First, propaganda must be disseminated and members recruited. Second, the authorities must be overcome in an area where 'there is a broad enough base to allow the resumption of Islamic life through the ideas of the party'. Finally, the Islamic state 'would begin forming an army whose function would be to oppose the armies of... [the godless states and] . . . bring about their overthrow and put Islamic rules into action.'[16]

Syria

Since 1976, President Hafez al-Asad of Syria has faced a popular Islamic challenge to the stability of his regime. Anti-government propaganda has been distributed, strikes organized, government officials assassinated, and other acts of armed opposition carried out. Such events reached a climax in February 1982 when a skirmish between security forces and members of the Muslim Brotherhood in the Syrian city of Hamah escalated into a city-wide uprising. Fighting raged for several days as the Syrian Army bombarded the city into submission, killing an estimated five thousand or more people in the process.[17]

A number of factors have contributed to the emergence of popular Islam as the primary opposition force in Syria. The first of these factors is political in nature: in Syria, as in Egypt and pre-revolutionary Iran,

Islam represents the only broadly understood and easily disseminated ideology upon which opposition to the status quo can be based. Other potential political forces are too esoteric for general consumption, have been discredited by past events, or have been co-opted by the ruling Ba'ath – or in some cases (such as the Syrian Communist Party) by all three. Popular Islam, on the other hand, utilizes readily-comprehensible symbols and is easily spread by a sympathetic clergy.[18]

A second factor contributing to the popular Islamic challenge in Syria is economic. Rapid industrialization and government policy have combined to threaten the economic viability of small traders in that country. This in turn has led many such individuals to adopt an Islamic defence of private property and their traditional livelihoods.[19]

Sectarian favouritism constitutes a third factor contributing to the growth of the popular Islamic opposition in Syria. Muslim organizations opposed to Asad have capitalized on the widespread dissatisfaction with the privileged position enjoyed by President Asad's Alawi co-religionists, and have warned members of Syria's Alawi community that 'nine to ten per cent of the population cannot be allowed to dominate the [Sunni] majority'.[20]

The leading role in the Islamic opposition to Asad in Syria has been taken by the Syrian branch of the Muslim Brotherhood, led by Adnan Sa'ad-al-Din, Sa'id Hawwa and others.[21] Other opposition Islamic organizations included the Islamic Liberation Party, the Islamic Liberation Movement, and the Youth of Muhammad.[22] In 1976, the deepening economic crisis, Syrian intervention in Lebanon, and the increasingly Alawite character of the regime, led the Brotherhood to declare a *jihad* against the Asad government.[23] Muslim Brotherhood membership rapidly grew (particularly among students) and violence against the government was intensified. In June 1979, eighty-three Alawi military cadets at the Aleppo Artillery Academy were killed (and many more wounded) in an attack launched by anti-government forces and aided by a disgruntled Sunni military officer. In June 1980, some four hundred or so people were killed during an attempted escape of political prisoners in Palmyra. The government responded in July 1980 with Law 49, which made Muslim Brotherhood membership a capital offence. Nevertheless, armed confrontation continued, with 1981 seeing a massive bomb attack against government installations in Damascus and 1982 seeing the uprising in Hamah.

Since late 1980, the Muslim Brotherhood has joined with other

Islamic organizations in the formation of the 'Islamic Front in Syria', the aim of which is the overthrow of the Asad regime and the establishment of an Islamic state based on the *Shari'a*.[24] In 1982, in the aftermath of the Hamah massacre, a National Alliance for the Liberation of Syria was formed, within which the Islamic Front (together with Nasserites, pro-Iraqi Ba'athists, and other opposition groups) played an active part.

North Africa

The triumph of the Iranian revolution in 1979 served to accelerate the growth of popular Islam as far afield as the Maghreb. In Tunisia, Algeria and Morocco, opposition to the government has increasingly been expressed in Islamic form, and dealing with the popular Islamic threat has become an important area of government policy.

The popular Islamic challenge to the status quo is particularly acute in Tunisia, where a domestic programme of modernization, a moderate Tunisian foreign policy, and high rates of domestic unemployment have combined to create a significant Islamic backlash, primarily manifest in the Islamic Tendency Movement. In July 1981, the Tunisian government arrested Islamic Tendency Movement leader Rashid Ghanouchi. Two months later, the *chador* (Islamic women's dress) was banned, in an attempt to limit the growth of popular Islam on Tunisian campuses. The Tunisian government also encouraged imams to refute the ideological position of the Islamic activist movements in their Friday sermons.[25] Further arrests occurred in 1983, and when major riots broke out in January 1984 over food price increases, President Habib Bourgiba placed much of the blame on the Movement, and more arrests of Islamic Tendency Movement members followed. In turn, the Movement accused the government of 'systematic corruption, ostentatious spending, repression of popular demands, torture, and mass imprisonment'.[26] Seventeen of those arrested were subsequently released by the government in August, amid tentative signs of a relaxation of tension between the two sides.[27]

Riots over food price increases also took place in Morocco in January 1984, and were attributed by King Hassan II to the subversive efforts of 'Khomeinists' (as well as 'Marxist-Leninists' and 'Zionists'). In Algeria the strength of popular Islamic sentiment was demonstrated on 13 March 1984 by the attendance of some 25,000 people at the funeral of Shaykh Abd al-Latif Soliani, an Islamic activist who had died while under house arrest.[28]

Perspective

The phenomenon of contemporary Islamic political activism is a product of the socio-economic, socio-political and socio-cultural conditions of the Islamic world. These conditions are manifested in the interrelated and multi-faceted crises of development, inequality and identity that have intensified over the century and produced war, oppression and dependency in their wake. An explanation of the rise of religious political activism lies in the failure of political systems to deal with these problems – indeed, minimally to safeguard the community against foreign domination and exploitation in its various forms. As revealed in the history of Islamic political thought, this has been viewed as the most basic obligation of government in Islamic society. It is significant that the two states where Islamic activism has been most pronounced and sustained – Iran and Egypt – are the two states where Western ideologies of development, the domination of Western cultural, economic and political influences, and the problem of foreign territorial occupation, have been most explicit.

While the many groups that have been examined as part of the contemporary Islamic political activist movement are diverse, there are a number of characteristics common to all of them. First, they are all committed to a *salafi* ideology. The normative characteristics of this are puritanical moralism, collectivism, and universalism. Second, the goals of the movement are politically reactionary in that the groups seek Islamification of political institutions as their primary objective. In the short term, this has meant a return to Islamic legal codes rigidly interpreted; in the longer term, a return to the ideal *Khalafah* of the Rashidun. They are usually organized around authoritarian leaders, with control highly centralized. Finally, in their methods, they all rely on zealous missionary tactics for recruitment and rigid ritual performance for maintenance. In the only case examined here where an Islamic activist group has successfully attained power – Iran – these features have been transported to public institutions.

Contemporary Islamic political activism has roots in the socio-cultural and socio-political traditions of Islam as manifested in the rich heritage of Islamic political thought. Indeed, the various groups that make up the movement use this body of knowledge, albeit highly selectively and particularistically, to legitimate their actions. While the movement is already fragmenting internally, as revealed in the case studies examined here, and its energies are increasingly dissipated with the in-fighting that accompanies this, it nevertheless has reasserted an Islamic frame of reference for the problems of political legitimacy and accountability. The Islamic political activist movement may merely be the harbinger of an Islamic ideological renaissance – a reawakening of the political values manifested in Islamic political thought and a search for institutions that represent these values.

Notes

1. Sadiq Jalal al-Azm, *Naqd al-Fikr al-Dini*, 2nd edn, Beirut, Dar al-Talia, 1970, p. 17.
2. Muammar al-Qaddafi, *The Green Book*, Ottawa, Jerusalem International Publishing House, 1983.
3. Marius K. Deeb and Mary Jane Deeb, *Libya Since the Revolution*, New York, Praeger, 1982, p. 102.
4. Quoted in John Wright, *Libya: A Modern History*, London, Croom Helm, 1981, pp. 185–6.
5. From an interview with Farouq Abu Issa, member of the Central Committee of the Sudanese Communist Party and member of the first cabinet after the Numayri coup of 1969. Cairo, 27 December 1984.
6. Alexander C. Cudsi, 'Islam and Politics in the Sudan', in James P. Piscatori (ed.), *Islam in the Political Process*, Cambridge, Cambridge University Press, 1983, p. 45.
7. Ibid.
8. Other Muslim Brethren, led by Sadiq Muhammed Ahd al-Majid, supported Islamification but opposed integration into the 'compromise structure' of the SSU. *Al-Majallah*, London, 15–21 October 1983, pp. 15–16.
9. Ja'far Muhammed Numayri, *al-Nahi al-Islami limatha*, Cairo, al-Maktab al-Misri al-Hadith, 1981.
10. *Al-Tadamun*, London, 14 July 1984, pp. 18–19.
11. *Al-Majallah*, London, 15–21 October 1983, pp. 15–16.
12. *The Journal of the Muslim World League*, Mecca, August 1980, pp. 27–31.
13. *Attadamon* 1, Paris, No. 40, 14 January 1984, pp. 27–29.
14. These include the Islamic Solidarity Fund; the Islamic Development Bank; the International Islamic News Agency; the Islamic States Broadcasting Organization; the Jerusalem Fund; the Islamic Red Crescent; the Islamic Organization for Science and Industry; the Islamic Science Foundation; the Islamic Centre for Development of Trade; the Islamic Relief Agency; the Islamic Chambers of Commerce and Industry; the Islamic Food Surety Fund; the Islamic Shipowners Association; the Organization of Islamic Capitals; the Islamic Universities in Niger and Uganda; and the Islamic Solidarity Games. See Hamid H. Kizilbash, 'The Islamic Conference Organization: Retrospect and Prospect', *Arab Studies Quarterly* 4, Nos. 1–2, 1982, p. 156.
15. In the 1979 and 1981 student elections at Bar Zeit University, for example, Islamic states won 43 and 35 per cent of the votes, respectively. See 'Munir Fasheh: Political Islam in the West Bank', *Merip Reports*, February 1982, pp. 15–17.

16. *Akhir Sa'ah*, Cairo, 3 August 1983, p. 14. *Al-Majallah*, London, 13–19 August 1983, p. 5. Ibrahim, 'Anatomy', p. 435.
17. Hanna Batatu, 'Syria's Muslim Brethren', *Merip Reports* 110, November–December 1982, p. 20.
18. Ibid., pp. 14–15.
19. Fred Lawson, 'The Social Bases for the Hama Revolt', *Merip Reports* 110, November–December 1982, pp. 24–8. Also see the provisions regarding private ownership in 'The Program of the Islamic Revolution' in Umar F. Abd-Allah, *The Islamic Struggle in Syria*, Berkeley, Mizan Press, 1983, p. 221.
20. 'Manifesto of the Islamic Revolution of Syria' in Ibid., pp. 210–11.
21. A split occurred in 1971 between this group and the followers of Syrian Muslim Brotherhood leader Isam al-Attar, who opposed armed confrontation with the Ba'athist regime. The former group won international Muslim Brotherhood recognition. The two wings were not reunited until 1981.
22. Michael C. Hudson, 'The Islamic Factor in Syrian and Iraqi Politics' in Piscatori (ed.), *Islam in the Political Process*, p. 85.
23. Abd-Allah, *The Islamic Struggle in Syria*, p. 109.
24. For a detailed examination of the Islamic Front, see Abd-Allah, *The Islamic Struggle in Syria*, pp. 114–88, and the 'Manifesto and Programs of the Islamic Front' in ibid., pp. 201–67.
25. *Al-Nahar al-'Arabi wa al-Duwali*, Paris, 31 December 1979–6 January 1980, pp. 20–2.
26. *Middle East Economic Digest*, 3–9 February 1984.
27. *Al-Ra'y*, Tunis, 10 August 1984.
28. *Le Monde*, Paris, 15–16 March 1984.

Part III

Appendix

Three Interviews and an Address

Qadhdafi on Islamic democracy

Interview with the Libyan Head of State Mo'amer Qadhdafi in Tripoli, September 1979, on the occasion of the tenth anniversary of the revolution, by Heinz Gastrein, Der Tagesspiegel, *West Berlin.*

Question: A decade ago, when you made Islam the guideline of your revolution in Libya, you were being laughed at by everybody. Since then, most of them are now laughing on the other side of their faces, particularly after what has recently happened in Iran. Does Khomeini's Islamic revolution appear to you as a confirmation of your own concept of an Islamic rejuvenation?

Answer: I would rather like to defer a final assessment of the Islamic revolution in Tehran. It is a significant aspect of this Iranian popular uprising that it could draw its strength from a rejuvenated, modern, progressive and revolutionary Islam which does not differentiate between Christians, Jews and Muslims.

Question: How is it possible that Islam, which believes itself to be the consummate monotheistic revealed religion, could suddenly cease to differentiate between its own faithful believers and Christians and Jews?

Answer: Libya is the unique example of a comprehensive revolution which offers itself to all mankind, to liberate man, whom the Qur'ān calls God's representative on earth, from all material and spiritual obstacles which hamper man's volition. Islam is nothing else but the humanistic revolution: an absolute faith in the forces of good and the capacities for good which are inherent in man, which enable man to overcome the consequences of injustice and aggression that have held man back in a state of backwardness and forces which enable man to advance on the road of progress. Thus, today's revolution of the Arab in the Libyan Jamahiriyah is a part of the world-wide Islamic movement which is fighting today to gain for itself its rightful place in the world after many centuries of darkness.

Question: Fighting? Is it then still a Holy War of Islam?

Answer: Since the Arab people of Libya remold their lives in the spirit of the noble Islamic legal order, the '*Shari'a*', it can only mean an all-Islamic brotherhood and solidarity as well as a return to a responsible use of the 'jihad', the Holy War, in the ways of Allah and of Islamic unity.

Question: Where do you use 'jihad' in a 'responsible' way?

Answer: We support the Muslim revolution in the Philippines since that revolution raised arms against terror, murder and gangs of racists. It was indeed our support which wrested from the Philippine government a readiness to acknowledge some Muslim rights and demands for autonomy. We equally stand behind the Islamic struggle in the United States.

Question: You have often pointed to the leading role of Libya in the Islamic world today. What is being undertaken in this direction?

Answer: We are helping primarily African Muslims build mosques and schools. We equip Islamic diaspora communities all over the world with Islamic books and stipends, provide teachers for Islamic and Arabic subjects and send missionaries. I would like to invite the Muslims of the world to send their sons to the Islamic colleges and institutes of the Libyan Jamahiriyah. The courses of Arabic and Islamic studies at Al-Beida already count among their students many Muslim students from Africa, Asia, the Far East and many other parts of the world.

Question: You have repeatedly directed calls for a policy of Islamic solidarity to the other Muslim countries. Solidarity in what respect and for what purpose?

Answer: To spread Islamic culture and oppose atheism; to remold everyday life so that it will conform again in actual practice to Islamic values, principles and moral postulates. To achieve Islamic co-operation in technology, science, education, and in the field of culture. To establish an Islamic economic organization to develop and consolidate the Islamic national economies making use of an Islamic bank as the principal instrument.

Question: How wonderful to be a Muslim today, but back again to your earlier assertion that there will be no differentiation, that is, no discrimination against Christians and Jews?

Answer: The doctrines of Islam demand that support be given to all who are weak, even to those who are not Muslims. The appeals of the needy must be heard. The Libyan Jamahiriyah is guided in all its activities by this doctrine.

Question: Is this then a general humanitarian attitude rather than a religious one? Can the same be said of your political ideology? Do you yourself consider your rule as 'Islamic divine right' or an 'Islamic republic' where all authority emanates from the people?

Answer: The fundamental laws in every society are based on tradition and religion. Every other attempt to impose on any society laws outside these two sources is unlawful and illogical. Constitutions are not laws of the society. A constitution is a man-made basic law. A law of this kind should have a source for its justification. The law of society, however, is an enduring human heritage which is not merely the property of the living generation.

Religion comprises the traditions which are an expression of the natural life of the people. In this way religion, comprising tradition, is a confirmation of natural law. Non-religious and non-traditional laws are inventions used by one man against another. They are therefore unlawful and not founded on the natural sources of tradition and religion.

As a successor to the era of republics, the age of the masses is approaching rapidly. It heralds joyfully the true freedom of peoples and their emancipation from the fetters of governmental instruments as it will also provide a shield against the approaching anarchy and demogogy. For this purpose the power of the individual, class, tribe, sect or party must be broken in order to have the new Islamic democracy become the direct power of the people.

Numayri on religious reforms

Interview with President Ja'far Numayri by Fu'ad Matar of al-Tadamun: *'The End of the World Might Start in Lebanon; As of Today, There Will Be No Imamate in the Sudan'.* Al-Tadamun, London, No. 31, 12 November 1983, pp. 6–12.

There is no one who knows like someone who has heard; there is no one who has heard like someone who has seen; there is no one who has seen like someone who has borne witness and debated.

A saying of this sort is essential as a starting point for describing the nature of this conversation with President Ja'far Numayri.

I had previously held some interviews with President Numayri, over a period of 10 years, but this interview occurred in the midst of circumstances which were distinctive and regarding which there were many statements and explanations. Perhaps the most prominent of these circumstances was that President Numayri surprised the Sudanese and others, while at the same time not surprising them, on the subject of the application of Islamic laws, and surprised them, or, for accuracy's sake, surprised some of them, in terms of timing but surprised no one in terms of preparation.

In addition to that, there is the mission which President Numayri does not cease striving to achieve, which bears on devising a conciliatory formulation for the restoration of relations between Egypt and the Arab countries.

During a week replete with meetings and discussions with a number of Sudanese brethren, the picture of the Islamic transformation became clearer. If one may say so, it now is possible to convey some impressions on what has happened and is still in the process of happening in the Sudan as a result of the application of Islamic laws, and it is also now possible to read these laws and the interpretations and theories which have accompanied them with a high degree of insight . . . .

What is particularly noteworthy in President Numayri's talk is his analysis of the struggle between American and Soviet strategy in the Middle East area. In the context of this analysis, he cited a phrase which draws the attention of the listener or reader. That phrase is 'The end of the world might start in Lebanon.' Also noteworthy in his conversation is his statement 'There will be no imamate as of now in the Sudan,' unless, as he expresses it, it is of al-Ghazali's sort of imamate, that is, an imamate of learning and jurisprudence.

'Al-Tadamun: Mr. President, you have adopted decrees that no regime after you will be able to abrogate, even if the Communists take power. However, only you can exercise enough flexibility to thwart many predictions and rumours. Will you exercise this flexibility?

President Ja'far Numayri: In the name of God the most merciful and all-compassionate; thanks and praise be to God, and prayers for his prophet and our messenger of God. The declaration of governance by Islamic law in the Sudan is a matter which goes beyond the Sudan and is of concern to the Arabs and Muslims in general. However, before going into details on it, let us recall this same date

(18 October 1964), when the Sudanese people sought the restoration of democratic life from the military regime, and to the role we played within the armed forces to support the popular upheaval which was crowned by victory on 21 October, when we went over to the side of the people and the military leaders were compelled to relinquish power in accordance with rules and principles we set forth. These remain the same principles and rules as those on whose basis we unleashed the 25 May 1969 revolution, after the civilians had failed to preserve the people's gains and had fallen prey to tribal, racial, factional and party disputes, which prompted us to move the armed forces, and the other military forces, toward greater national action and the development of their role in an alliance with the working forces of the people, so that with the power they had, they became the organization, will and solidarity of the force leading this alliance, causing the citizens to insist on electing an individual from the armed forces to be a president for a third term, being totally convinced that this was not a military regime, as others alleged, although the President engages in all his official activities in military uniform.

Question: What happened during this period of government?

Answer: What happened was that the principles and policies which I have been assigned and have committed myself to have been carried out. In response to your question on our decision to be governed by God's book, I would like to remind people of the first communiqué of the revolution, the communiqués which I have declared in all my meetings, the national charter which we wrote, the constitution and the various laws. In all these documents there is a clear orientation toward government by God's book and the commitment to Islamic law. In a nation in which Islamic culture is extremely deep-rooted, we raised government by the book from the level of the individual to that of the government, Muslims are to govern themselves by God's book, a matter which has enabled this country, with numerous cultures (550 tribes or more) and a vast area (2.5 million square kilometres), to live in peace and security, in comparison with the bordering countries. The declaration of government by Islamic law in the Sudan was not a surprise to most of the citizens, but the surprise for us was embodied in the rapid positive response and the happiness and joy with which it was met not just domestically but abroad as well, and by citizens in countries with which we are not linked by good relations, such as Iran and Libya.

The religious compunctions of the Sudanese citizen are very

strong. Even people who drink liquor were gladdened by the decree prohibiting it, and specialists in economic affairs did not react favourably to statements that there would be a deficit in revenues from the customs and production duties imposed on alcohol. The only person who raised this matter with me was the representative of the International Monetary Fund, who told me that the decree would create a gap of 40 million pounds in revenues. I answered him that I had not imagined that it would be more than 4 million, but if it was truly 40 million that supported the decree and made it necessary, and it would be possible to make sacrifices domestically which would cover this gap. In addition, prohibiting liquor would save us the money we spend on citizens for its health effects, as well as its negative social features.

We received many cables and letters from families and women praising the decree, which gave them back their social well-being. You may observe the approval of public opinion from the comments and cartoons the newspapers are publishing. The only difficulty which faced me from the standpoint of execution of these decrees was that they were not carried out with the necessary speed to quickly achieve the goal of restoring the rights to the people and making justice the arbitrator.

Western countries accuse us of barbarism regarding Islamic provisions and ignore that Islamic provisions are more merciful, and that execution to us is not murder, as it is to them, since it is possible to substitute blood money for the family of the person murdered, indeed, the family of the person murdered can pardon the murderer.

The British Ambassador and the Experts

Al-Tadamun: Have some ambassadors addressed themselves to the question of foreign experts or asked that specific exceptions be allotted to them?

President Ja'far Numayri: Many foreigners and diplomats may perhaps not realize that Islam was revealed to serve man and that all its legislation has the goal of regulating family, social and individual life and raising the level of the individual. When we declared the prohibition on alcohol, the British ambassador came to me with a general from his country who was visiting the Sudan, and found the opportunity to tell me that the decree might perhaps result in the loss of foreign experts. I told him that if the reason for the presence of advisers in the Sudan was alcohol, let us lose them; there are many people on earth who do not like alcohol. Indeed, the Christian religion does not encourage the drinking of alcohol. I told him that I had expected he would be bringing us a letter of thanks from his government, because we have about 4,000 British experts here whom the decree will help cure of the problems of alcohol. I told him, 'You are fighting smoking, which is a stimulant, so what about alcohol? In any event, it is always the duty of foreigners to observe the laws of the country in which they live.' The ambassador was won over by what I said.

Some people talk about the condition of women and say that I will issue republican decrees imposing the veil on women. I object to the word 'veil', because to veil something means hiding it from existence. Women here participate in the society. By their nature they are against flagrant dress. The Sudanese robe, which is part of our culture, is adequate for us here; women in the era of the prophet pursued working careers. Our Lady Khadijah worked in trade.

Al-Tadamun: Did you familiarize yourself with a report, a memorandum or a study on alcohol in the Sudan from the financial and health standpoints before adopting the decision?

President Ja'far Numayri: Of course. We subject all laws to thorough study before approving them. There were specialized committees of a number of scholars from the Sudan and abroad who set out the formulation of some laws for us; we familiarized ourselves with them, amended them, and added the Islamic penalties to them.

Al-Tadamun: Now that it is being applied, will you ask for a study on the psychological effects that have arisen from prohibition?

President Ja'far Numayri: Actually, we have not done so. However, we have followed up and have statistics departments which present regular reports on the effects of laws on individuals and groups. Fortunately, all the reports have been extremely encouraging.

Al-Tadamun: Is it permissible to assume that there was an element of conscience or a position of a personal character on your excellency's part in these decrees?

President Ja'far Numayri: I can say that there was an element of conscience, perhaps as an effect of my religious upbringing. Also, my personal experience with alcohol has been of influence in convincing me of its harmful and ill effects.

Al-Tadamun: Some people wonder if you will compel people to keep the fast of Ramadan, for instance?

President Ja'far Numayri: Any Muslim who has attained the conditions of a Muslim, in the sense that he has attained maturity, must commit himself to the rituals of worship, unless there are legitimate reasons and authorizations that exempt him from that. I do not compel people to fast, but I do compel them not to break the fast openly. I do not compel them to pray, but I do offer the wherewithal for guidance and good exhortation, in carrying out the dictum that there is no compulsion in religion.

Al-Tadamun: What stages did these decrees go through? Are they a summary of experience in governing or are they a state of religious worship?

President Ja'far Numayri: I can say that they are a mixture of both. From the standpoint of experience in governing, I affirmed that the secular laws did not solve the problems of the society and the individual. From the standpoint of worship, these laws were the radical solution to these problems, and some Islamic laws which were applied, such as the personal status laws, were the object of people's approval. The only problem was the delay in resolving cases.

The gradual way in which these laws were set out was a factor. When our brother al-Rashid al-Tahir was prime minister in 1967, he assigned a committee of Arab and Muslim scholars to set out a plan for Islamic laws, and some of them actually were prepared and presented to the national People's Assembly 5 years ago but not discussed. Last year, I drew one of them out of the assembly and issued it as a temporary order to set an example for the deputies. This year I felt that I had to act alone, and issued these laws. They met with approval from the members of the People's Assembly, who are now setting out a plan to approve them rapidly.

Al-Tadamun: Some people have observed, from photographs of the act of destroying the liquor, that you were breaking bottles as if they were sea monsters, or enemies. What is the story behind that?

President Ja'far Numayri: Perhaps this is the result of my view of alcohol as the greatest of vices and one of the major reasons for our backwardness. Perhaps this is the reason colonialism encouraged it. Even the leading colonial figures indicated that it was wholesome.

And restrictions on smoking

Al-Tadamun: In the context of further guidance, could the situation reach the point where the phenomenon of smoking, which is widespread throughout the Sudan, would be restricted?

President Ja'far Numayri: After we affirmed that smoking is seriously harmful to health, we started to do so. In this regard we issued a law aimed at putting pressure on smokers, for instance prohibiting smoking in public places and enclosed rooms. We raised the customs duties on it, increasing its prices. There has been an improvement in this direction, since many people have reduced the rate at which they smoke. In the future we will stop the cultivation of tobacco, in order to combat smoking.

Al-Tadamun: On your recent decrees, specifically with regard to the prohibition on alcohol, connected to what you called in the past 'upright leadership', and your famous letter to Sudanese civilian and military officials, what were the circumstances behind the sending of this letter?

President Ja'far Numayri: The directives which I addressed earlier to leaders were part of the gradual process of arriving at a decree prohibiting alcohol in the case of all citizens, on grounds that the leaders are the models and must be examples for the people below them. This letter realized good results; the overwhelming majority of the leaders responded to it, and that encouraged me to take other steps. The leaders themselves also encouraged the sending of similar letters to their subordinates, and that met with a dazzling response.

During the act of destroying the liquor in the Nile, we observed that Christian religious figures and some other non-Muslim religious sects were in the front ranks, and they were happy with this action.

I would like to add that we have embarked on a new experience in the military forces; 31 officers of different ranks are to graduate from the Islamic Centre tomorrow after a year of religious study to work as givers of sermons in mosques belonging to the armed forces. This is an experience in whose results I have confidence. It is the first one in the realm of combining military discipline and religious commitment, and the development of Islamic culture in the ranks of the military forces, to make personnel honest, sincere and moral, and have them avoid trumping up charges against people fraudulently. I can remember that President Jamal 'Abd-al-Nasir called for that sort of thing. In the Suez War of 1956, every soldier had a copy of the holy Qur'ān, and there also was a priest in the midst of the combatants. The July revolution's first national anthem was the anthem 'God is Great'.

The south and Ethiopia

Al-Tadamun: Citizens in the southern Sudan feel great appreciation for you personally. Do you expect that these decrees will cause grumbling in their ranks, because of their diversity and their own circumstances, and that they will demand that they be exempted from them?

President Ja'far Numayri: Our brothers in the south do indeed honour their president, and they know me personally. I have worked with them a great deal since and have had much experience with them, and that has helped bring me closer to them.

Some long-standing politicians believe that the south could be the avenue for an invasion of the Sudan. Therefore they have acted, along with some other countries like Libya and Ethiopia, which recently joined the camp that is hostile to us, out of its belief that enmity toward Khartoum can solve its own problems in Eritrea, and therefore started to co-operate with Libya and build bases to oppose us. We have much information, but we also have the hope that Ethiopia will retreat from its position. We do not want to take a position of enmity toward Ethiopia, and we hope that it will get out of the enemy camp which it has joined, and indeed the Eastern camp in general. Hostile elements have imagined that the recent decrees have been an opportunity to stir up the people in the south, and have unfortunately started to co-ordinate with some churches. They have started making it appear to the world that there is an opposition and resistance in southern circles. This is international hostility toward Islam. I cannot stop it, but I can prevent its influence in the Sudan, without fanaticism, terror or the use of force.

Tolerance, strictness and the reduction in embassies

Al-Tadamun: Concerning domestic issues, there are three points. The first is on the new climate, and whether that will make you more tolerant or strict in dealing with domestic matters. The second is related to the great reduction in the Sudan's embassies abroad, and the third concerns a ministry of the utmost delicacy and sensitivity, the Ministry of Energy, which is headed by a person who is considered to adhere to a specific political orientation.

President Ja'far Numayri: With respect to tolerance or strictness, I believe that it is the style of leadership that determines that. My style of leadership is that I rely more on my personal abilities which God has given me than on power, bills or laws. I believe that the passage of Islamic legislation itself will fail if the leader wants to use it and derive his power from it alone, because the reasons for the passage of Islamic legislation are clear. It has the goal of raising the individual and providing a deterrent for the group; we must use the punishment of the individual to provide a deterrent for the group.

I do not believe that I will be strict unless the meaning of strictness is self-control. I will stop the wrongdoer where he is, so that others may take warning. Tolerance is not appropriate, either, because tolerance means laxity, and the purpose of the laws is to stop laxity.

As far as the second point goes, the reduction in the embassies was made in the context of the slogan of reducing government spending and in a framework of programmes and study . . . .

Al-Sadat addresses religious scholars and notables

President al-Sadat met with the Muslim ulama in the fall of 1979 in Ismailia. The meeting was attended by the Vice-President, Dr 'Abd-al-Rahman Bisar; the Sheikh of al-Azhar; Hasan al-Tuhami, the Deputy Prime Minister for the Presidence; Dr Sufi Abu-Talih, the People's Assembly speaker; Mansur Hasan, the Minister of State for the Presidency, and a large number of al-Azhar ulama and Muslim writers and thinkers. The following are excerpts from the President's address:

In the name of God, His eminence the grand imam and the venerable and esteemed brother ulema: I have invited you tonight so that we may discuss the question of rebuilding Egypt now that God, may He be praised, has opened our country to us. This country has become ours and there is no decision other than our decision and no will other than our will in it. You have heard your brothers and sisters from the various fields of specialization who spoke previously about the solutions and the problems that we are facing and for which we are all exerting efforts to reach solutions.

Our problems are complex because a long time passed during which numerous issues were neglected. We were then surprised by a population increasing by one million persons every year. We were surprised by all these problems facing us all at once. You have heard your brothers and sisters describe these problems and the solutions for them. Perhaps this is the first time in which we sit together like a single family, without distinction between ruler and ruled and as dictated by our tolerant religion, to discuss matters and to apply the words of God, may He be praised: 'They consult on their affairs.' . . . [Sadat discusses the pre- and post-independence history of Egypt. He concludes by stating:]

This is what God has willed for us, namely that faith constitute the primary and the firmest component of the personality of man on this land. And before that?

Al-Azhar and Islam

We must point out that al-Azhar remained the defender of Islam for a full 1,000 years. Had it not been for al-Azhar and for al-Azhar's battles – not only in Egypt but in all parts of the Islamic world – Islam would not have been able to triumph against the ferocious onslaught of the European colonialism which infiltrated Asia, Africa and our Arab area and attempted to strike Islam. This is because Islam has been and will continue to be a revolution – a revolution in every sense of the word. We are proud of this and we must be proud of it.

Story of Morocco conference

When the conferees met in Morocco a few months ago in an Islamic conference to which I had called . . . [sentence incomplete]. Perhaps you don't know this but the call to the Islamic conference which was held in Morocco a month or two ago came originally from me to the King of Morocco, asking him to call for the convocation of an Islamic conference in Morocco on the issue of Jerusalem. The King of Morocco cannot deny this and the Saudis cannot deny it. The call came originally from Egypt. I asked the King of Morocco in an official message, which I demand that he publish immediately to all, to call for the Islamic conference on Jerusalem. What has happened? What happened is that the ministers of foreign affairs met in Morocco and that while we were preparing to send the Egyptian delegation, the King of Morocco plotted with his minister of foreign affairs, the Saudis and the rejectionists to ban Egypt from attending that conference.

They feared the presence of the Egyptian delegation and feared that the Egyptian delegation would answer them and tell them that we were the originators and the ones who called for this conference and not Morocco, Saudi Arabia or any other country. They plotted and the matter ended with the suspension of Egypt's membership in the Islamic conference in the absence of Egypt – a suspension that came about as a result of Saudi bribes to some Arab countries at times and as a result of pressure exerted out of courtesy for Saudi Arabia at other times. But the Islamic African countries were eager to denounce this attitude and they recorded their denunciation and disapproval in the minutes of the conference.

Does suspending Egypt's membership eliminate Egypt's Islamic responsibility? Not at all. Does suspending Egypt's membership cancel what al-Azhar has done to preserve Islam for a 1,000 years against the ferocious colonialist attacks from one end of the world to the other? Does suspending Egypt's membership cancel this role? Not at all. Does suspending Egypt's membership abolish the fact that Egypt, after Mecca, is the point to which every Muslim in the world turns his eyes? It does not abolish that fact at all.

Responsibility

I wanted to mention this to you so that we may know what responsibility we face these days with you. I am not talking about food security, not about the housing problem, not about the infrastructures and not about what we are suffering because plans are being made for these issues by particular people. These plans will be presented to you, and to the entire people, in your capacity as being responsible not only for Islam but also for whatever concerns your homeland, your people and your future generations. I am talking about your primary responsibility toward Islam and toward the call for Islam. I begin by saying this and by telling the entire world that we know our Islamic responsibilities and we are aware of them, and so are numerous Islamic peoples in Africa and Asia and many Arab peoples who have not been pleased with the actions of their rulers. What has happened has been due to no reason other than malice against Egypt, against Egypt's status and against what Egypt has attained.

True Islam is here

We need to remember this and I mention it at the outset of my address to you because as a result I will ask you to state your opinion on this and on what has caused Egypt's Islamic role to be involved in these trivialities to which Saudi Arabia and those who follow its course and run behind it, namely Morocco [have led]. I want you to state your opinion on this. They say that Islam in Egypt is in danger. All of you here are men of the Islamic call.

Within earshot of the entire world, I say that we are proud that the true Islam is here in Egypt. Egypt is the island of freedom, democracy and man's dignity as desired by Islam. There isn't in Egypt a ruler who gets a salary of 8 million pounds of the money of Muslims. There isn't in Egypt a ruler who spends money on gambling tables while Muslims in many parts of the world are suffering. There isn't in Egypt a ruler who spends the money of Muslims on plotting, bribery and baseness just to build an imaginary leadership. Not at all. We in Egypt are fully aware of the limits. What have all those who spoke before me today demanded? Further application of the Islamic *Shari'a* and further adherence to the faith. But I ask: What is the situation of the peoples of those rulers? Not only the Islamic peoples in the remotest parts of the world are in need of help but so are the peoples of these rulers. Do these peoples truly enjoy the dignity of the Muslim citizen in his country? Without excluding a single one of these countries, the Muslim there does not enjoy the full dignity of the Muslim, the full dignity of the human being and the full democracy and tolerance, that are advocated by Islam, as they are enjoyed by the Muslim here . . . .

Faith

In the Ramadan battle of 1973, our weapons were 20 steps behind the Israeli weapons. What made up for those 20 steps and made our weapons more advanced [potent] than our enemies' weapons at that time? One word – faith. On these shores that extend 180 kilometres from Port Said to Suez and on the canal bank and when the Egyptian air force flew over [to the Israeli side] at 14.00 on 10 Ramadan, our sons did not await the orders to cross but their multitudes rushed forward along 180 kilometres from Port Said to the Suez chanting one call: God is great. This is true and not a tale that we tell with embellishments or claims of something that never happened. This did happen. We were 20 steps behind Israel in peace but with faith we got 20 steps ahead . . . .

We should start building the Egyptian youth from within. This is why I have asked that religion constitute a fundamental discipline – a discipline that determines success and failure – as of the beginning of the next academic year. I have also asked that religion be taught from the elementary stage to the university stage. There will be no trace of [wavering] in this. All I demand is that our methods be developed. I heard my daughters study Qur'an phrases and I asked them to memorize them. I tell you that I thank God today. I am celebrating not only meeting with you so that we may apply the principle of consultation and so that we may begin a new phase with a totally new state, but I also thank God that I concluded [memorizing] the Qur'an today. We the peasants are accustomed to celebrating the day on which the Qur'an [memorization] is concluded the way we celebrate any holiday or religious occasion. Rather, this day is a bigger celebration.

Conclusion of Qur'ān

I thank God that I have concluded today. I thank God, may He be praised, that He has enabled me to read the Qur'ān and to begin my education and my life with memorizing the Qur'ān. This is why I tell you that when my daughters showed me the phrases they were required to memorize [I found that] they are among the most difficult phrases of the Qur'ān to read – why I remember 1927; I will never forget it. It was 1927 and I was at the beginning of my elementary school. Teaching us the Qur'ān started with the easy and understandable stories of the prophets. These stories open up – by their quality – the horizons of imagination before the child. A child is full of imagination in this stage. So, let us provide him with what nourishes his imagination and gives him the first joys of the future religious education. We have not forgotten until this moment the day in which our teacher told us the story of the angels who opened the chest of the prophet, may God's peace and prayers be upon him, one day after he had taken his sheep to pasture, got the devil out of it and then washed the chest. Some westernized people or those who call themselves rationalists, philosophers or atheists may cast doubt on this story. But the fact remains that since the day I was told this story when I was a child in the first years of my life, I learned that there is good and there is evil, that there is a devil that dwells in man's heart, that man should rid himself of this devil or should make sure that this devil does not control his actions. This is why I demand that religious teaching start at the elementary stage with the stories of the prophets. We have among our esteemed education professors those who can do better in this direction than what I am saying or do more to achieve this goal. I may [not be very well versed] on this issue and I just wanted to give you an example.

True Islam

In the fundamental components, we should also teach our children that God, may He be praised, is right, that good is right, that justice and whatever makes life honourable is right and that venerating parents is right. You cannot imagine how annoyed I was after 18 January when I invited the Federation of University Students. The federation [delegation] included a youth who had grown a beard as if to tell us that he had reached the epitome of piety. You remember that he was uncouth and loathsome. Does Islam consist of uncouthness and foulness? Does not Islam teach love, gentle words and faith which make a human being balanced in all his life and which opens his heart and his soul to people and to everything? This, not foulness, is Islam. Regrettably, this student comes from among those who have grown their beards and who have led the religious societies about which they talk in the universities . . . .

In whose interest is this?

'Umar al-Talmasani issues the [Islamic Brotherhood magazine – *Al-Da'wah*] with a front-page article saying that Mamduh Salim received a message from the U.S. administration or the U.S. intelligence telling him: Beware and watch the Islamic groups. They are very dangerous. Strike them and get rid of them. Is this true? This method made me so sad and it must end. After all that happened in the past, 'Umar – as you yourself exactly said – and after I opened all the jails and detention camps, rehabilitated you, established the supremacy of the law and gave full freedom [you still write this]. You mention a magazine and nobody objects, even though the publication of this magazine is illegal and should be stopped immediately. Not at all. But in whose interest? The youth? What I say is that we should accept the challenge and build for Egypt the great Islamic structure which starts with man over whom there is no power other than the power of God, may He be praised. How can I [you] say that the United States sent a frightening message? How can I [you] depict the Egyptian government which has given all this [freedom] as a government that receives [instructions] from the United States or from others telling it to round up the Islamic groups? This is sabotage. It sabotages our youth who will imagine, regrettably, that these statements contain the truth. Don't you remember the time when there was semi-Soviet intervention before I prepared for my battle and when I was in the direst need of the Soviet Union to supply me with arms to wage my battle, when my relations with the United States were severed and when I was attacking the United States violently? At that time, there was suspicion that they [Soviets] wanted to interfere and I ordered 17,000 Soviet experts to leave Egypt within a week. I set the deadline and 24 hours before that deadline, the Soviets carried out the order. I want us to build our youths on right, strength and truth and not on rumours. I also want the course of the Muslim Brotherhood to be different from its past course before 23 July [1952] . . . .

This should not be repeated

This is why I want this to be the conduct of every one of us who deals with religion and who teaches religion to our future generations. As a result of this – of the old course – I demand that this course not be

followed again because I will block it before the people. I do not do'
things behind closed doors. I do everything in the open. As a result of
this [old course], young kids attacked the Technical Military [College],
as you know, and slaughtered its guards like sheep in the name of
religion – in the name of religion. They were Muslim Brothers. They
were one of the branches that emerged from the Muslim Brotherhood.
Shukry Mustafa assassinated Dr al-Dahabi. Who of us did not
condemn what happened to Dr al-Dahabi. This is shameful. Shukry
Mustafa was originally a Muslim Brother. I am taking this opportunity
to speak frankly before you as the man in charge . . .

Islamic groups

This is why I am speaking frankly. Now some so-called Islamic groups
have emerged with calls that mislead our sons. In whose interest is
their deception? If we want to give our children lessons from history,
then let us give them complete and undiminished lessons and not
have some people who focus on the tender youth to incite them, and
they are by their nature easy to incite and instigate, against this or that.
Matters with the Islamic groups have reached the point where one of
their members went to tell his father: The money you take from the
state is illicit and I don't want your money. Their acts then turned into
crimes. You heard me say in al-Minya and Asyut that these groups
burn [newspaper] kiosks and that some of them enter the auditoriums
and kick out the professors to stop teaching. Is this Islam? They saw a
man walking with his daughter in al-Minya and said to him: How can
you walk with a girl? He answered: This is my daughter. So, they asked
him for a birth certificate [to prove that she was his daughter]. God,
may He be praised, said to Muhammad: 'You will not control them.
Call to your God's path with wisdom and exhortation'.

I am taking this opportunity to tell you all that is in my heart because
after this I will not, by God, have mercy [for crimes committed in the
name of] Islam and religion. I can never put the interest of the group
and of Egypt in a balance with which the likes of such people tamper.
They push matters too far. A young kid from al-Minya belonging to
these groups was printing pamphlets in Cairo. When he was seized, he
had in his possession 800 pounds and pamphlets full of attacks on the
regime and the state. I am saying this after having told you about the
challenge we are facing, both domestically or externally. At home, we
have to solve the difficult problems and externally, we have to face,
regrettably, our brothers, put them in their place and teach them what
Egypt is. But first we must set ourselves aright from within.

No religion in politics

This is why I have declared that there is no religion in politics and no politics in religion. Some tried to exploit these words. I will now repeat them: No religion in politics and no politics in religion. For anybody who wants to engage in political action, the parties are present and so let him proceed and exercise his full right. But for religion to be exploited to pounce on the state or to attack the state, no. This is shameful. This is why there are numbers of imams – some of whom, brother 'Umar, are Muslim Brothers and some supporters of the Muslim Brotherhood – who use the mosques to attack the state.

State will not be tolerant

Let them know that the state will not be tolerant with anybody from now on. I owe you advice and I have given it to you and I owe you a chance and I have given it to you. The responsibilities facing us at home and abroad require us, as I have told you, to strike this deviation – to strike it. I ask you to strike it. You must strike it with your conduct first and by teaching our children, secondly, the sound facts about our history, our religion, our efforts and our work . . . .

Zayid on Islam and government

Interview with President Sheikh Zayid of the United Arab Emirates, by the Voice *review of London.*

Islam is the foundation

Question: What is the Islamic religion's influence on your life?
Answer: Islam is the foundation of whatever we believe in, do, or say. The Arabs achieved glory and honour after they repudiated their paganism and embraced Islam.
   Orthodox Islam requires every Muslim to serve his brother and co-operate with him, irrespective of his nationality or belief.
   We are proud of the teachings of Islam which emphasize justice, equality, and love.

Loyalty and service in the people's interest

Question: You have, Your Highness, made several visits to many Arab states. What is your opinion on the government systems which are followed in them: republican, monarchical, or presidential? And what is your opinion on the so-called Islamic socialism?

Answer: The foundations of a system are truth, loyalty, and service in the interest of the people and the country.

Terms are being used without any real meaning. Today, we find some people call others 'reactionary', 'progressive', or 'socialist'. Many use these terms for a purpose or an interest in themselves. Rarely, indeed, do we find a person who says the truth and applies it irrespective of any interest or benefit.

When a person tells another that he is a reactionary, what does he mean? Reaction in Arabic means a person who renounces and forsakes Islam. But this term is now being used in another sense.

Feeling in the heart of every Muslim

Question: The United Arab Emirates is witnessing an accelerated cultural and material progress. Can it, in spite of this progress, protect its Islamic principles and values?

Answer: As a matter of fact, there is no difference or conflict between the principles of Islam and progress. The contrary is the truth. Islam urges education, knowledge, and progress.

Question: The European countries have started to abandon the principles of Christianity as a result of the material progress they have achieved. This is tangible, especially with respect to the new generations. What is the situation in the Arab world?

Answer: Because of the circumstances through which the Arab world has passed, some people have neglected the teachings of orthodox Islam. But the great majority of the Arab people today believe in the Islamic heritage and that there is no glory, honour, or pride without Islam. I am sure that this feeling exists in the heart of every Muslim. That is why we now see Islam once again flourishing and getting stronger.

Question: What are your impressions of Arab nationalism? Is it derived from Islam?

Answer: Islam calls for closed ranks, coherence, and unity which are considered to be among the pillars of orthodox Islam. This does not mean that the coherence of the Muslim countries must isolate them from other countries and religions. The contrary is the truth. May the Almighty God be praised for he created us on this earth and made us equal. By his will he created us of different races and religions. The teachings of our religion call for co-operation with every human being, regardless of his religion.

Question: Your Highness, do you derive your rule from the teachings
of Islam?

Answer: Without doubt. We abide in all our deeds by the teachings of
orthodox Islam.

People's participation in government responsibility

Question: Do you believe in the importance of the people's
participation in government responsibility?

Answer: Yes, I believe in this. I believe in the necessity of the people's
participation in bearing responsibility, in counsel, and in government. Our aim in life is to promote justice and right, and to support
the weak against the strong. There is nothing to make us wary of our
people's participation in government responsibility as long as these
are our aims. We feel that it is our duty to distribute the
responsibilities to our people. We have actually done this. And
Islam calls for true democracy and justice.

Question: What are the qualities with which man must adorn
himself? And what are those which he must avoid?

Answer: I believe that the worst qualities are pride and arrogance.
The Qur'ān repudiates these qualities. Pride means disdaining
others. The fate of the proud and the arrogant is fire. Man must be
humble, and he must love his brothers and co-operate with them . . . .

Select Bibliography

In addition to the works cited in the text, the following are highly recommended.

Abdalatif, Hammudah, *The Structure of the Family in Islam*, Indianapolis, American Trust Publications, 1976.

'Abduh, Muhammad, *The Theology of Unity*, trans. Ishaq Musa' and Kenneth Cragg, New York, Books for Libraries, 1980.

Abu Saud, Mahmoud, 'Islamic Banking – The Dubai Case', *Outlines of Islamic Proceedings of the First Symposium on the Economics of Islam in North America*, Indianapolis, Association of Muslim Social Scientists, 1977

Ahmen, Khurshid, (ed.), *Studies in Islamic Economics*, Leicester, The Islamic Foundation, 1980.

al Faruqi, Ismai'il R., (ed.), *Historical Atlas of the Religions of the World*, New York, Macmillan, 1974.

——, *Islam and the Problem of Israel*, London, Islamic Council of Europe, 1980.

Al-Shirazi, Sadr al-Din, *The Wisdom of the Throne, An Introduction to the Philosophy of Mulla Sadra*, introduction, translation and notes by James Winston Morris, Princeton Library of Asian Translation, Princeton, Princeton University Press, 1981.

Arberry, Arthur J., *Aspects of Islamic Civilization*, Ann Arbor, Mich., University of Michigan Press, 1967.

Arnold, Thomas W., *The Preaching of Islam: A History of Propagation of the Muslim Faith*, New York, AMS Press (reprint of 1913 edn), first published in 1896. Also available in editions published by Kazi Publications and Orientalia.

Azzam, Abd-al-Rahman, *The Eternal Message of Muhammad*, Old Greenwich, Conn., Devin-Adair, 1964.

Azzam, S., (ed.), *The Muslim World and the Future Economic Order*, London, Islamic Council of Europe, 1979.

Baali, Fuad and Ali Wardi, *Ibn Khaldun and Islamic Thought-Styles: A Social Perspective*, Boston, G.K. Hall and Co., 1981.

Beck, L. and Keddie, N., (eds), *Women in the Muslim World*, Cambridge, Mass., Harvard University Press, 1978.

Beling, W.A., (ed.), *King Faisal and the Modernization of Saudi Arabia*, Boulder, Co., Westview Press, 1980.

Berger, M., *Islam in Egypt: Social and Political Aspects of Popular Religion*, New York, Cambridge University Press, 1970.

Brocklemann, Carl, *History of the Islamic Peoples*, New York, Putnam, 1960.

Bucaille, Maurice, *The Qur'ān* and the Bible, Indianapolis, American Trust Publications, 1978.

Charnay, Jean-Paul, *Sociologie religieuse de l'Islam*, Paris, Sindbad, 1977.

Chittick, William C., (ed.), *A Shiite Anthology*, Albany, State University of New York Press, 1981.

Cudsi, A.S. and Dessouki, Ali E. Hillal, *Islam and Power*, London, Croom Helm, 1981.

Dawisha, Adeed, (ed.), *Islam and Foreign Policy*, New York, Cambridge University Press, 1984.

Dessouki, Ali E. Hillal, (ed.), *Islamic Resurgence in the Arab World*, New York, Praeger, 1982.

Enayat, Hamid, *Modern Islamic Political Thought*, London, Macmillan, 1982.

Esposito, J.L., (ed.), *Islam and Development Religion and Sociopolitical Change*, Syracuse, NY, Syracuse University Press, 1980.

——, (ed.), *Voices of Resurgent Islam*, New York, Oxford University Press, 1983.

Gauhar, A., (ed.), *The Challenge of Islam*, London, Islamic Council of Europe, 1978.

Geertz, Clifford, Geertz, Hildred and Rosen, Lawrence, *Meaning and Order in Moroccan Society: Three Essays in Cultural Analysis*, New York, Cambridge University Press, 1979.

Gellner, Ernest, *Muslim Society – A Sociological Interpretation*, New York, Cambridge University Press, 1981.

Gibb, H.A., *Modern Trends in Islam*, Chicago, The University of Chicago Press, 1947.

Gibb, H.A. and Kramers, J.H., (eds), *Shorter Encyclopaedia of Islam*, Ithaca, NY, Cornell University Press, 1953.

Grube, Ernst J., *The World of Islam*, New York, McGraw-Hill, 1967.

Haddad, Yvonne Yazbeck, *Contemporary Islam and the Challenge of History*, Albany, NY, State University of New York Press, 1982.

Hamidullah, Muhamed, *Introduction to Islam*, Beirut, The Holy Koran Publishing House, 1977.

Hanafi, Hassan, *Religious Dialogue and Revolution*, Cairo, Anglo–Egyptian Bookshop, 1977.

Hassan, Hassan Ibrahim, *Islam: A Religious, Political, Social and Economic Study*, Beirut, Khayats, 1967.

Haykal, Muhammad Husayn, *The Life of Muhammad*, Indianapolis, American Trust Publications, 1976.

Hitti, Philip K., *History of the Arabs*, 10th edn, New York, St. Martin's Press, 1970.

Holy Qur'ān, The, trans. A. Yussef Ali, Indianapolis, American Trust Publications, is recommended. Also recommended are M. Marmaduke Pickthall's translation, *The Meaning of the Glorious Koran*, New York, New American Library (Mentor Books), and Arthur Arberry's translation, *The Koran Interpreted*, New York, Macmillan, 1964.

Jafri, S. Husain M., *Origins and Early Development of Shi'a Islam*, London, Longman, 1979.

Jamali, Mohammed F., *Letters on Islam: Written by a Father in Prison to His Son*, New York, Oxford University Press, 1965.

Jansen, G.H., *Militant Islam*, New York, Harper & Row, Torchbooks Library Binding, 1979.

Khadduri, Majid, *Arab Personalities in Politics*, Washington, DC, The Middle East Institute, 1981.

——, *Political Trends in the Arab World*, Baltimore, Johns Hopkins Press, 1970.

Kissinger, Henry A., *Years of Upheaval*, Boston, Little, Brown, 1982.

Kuhnel, Ernest, *Islamic Art and Architecture*, trans. Katherine Watson, Ithaca, NY, Cornell University Press, 1966.

Lewis, B. and Schacht, J., (eds), *Encyclopaedia of Islam*, 5 vols, Atlantic Highlands, NJ, Humanities Press, 1960.

Mahdi, Muhsin, *Ibn Khaldun's Philosophy of History*, Chicago, The University of Chicago Press, 1957.

Murray, J.P., 'Socialism in Islam: A Study of Algeria with a Translation of Excerpts from the Algerian National Charter', *Studies in Theoretical History*, 1981.

Moazzam, Anwar, *Islam and the Contemporary Muslim World*, New Delhi, Light and Life Publishers, 1981.

Nasr, Seyyed Hossein, *Ideals and Realities of Islam*, Boston, Beacon Press, 1972.

——, *Islamic Life and Thought*, Albany, NY, State University of New York Press, 1981.

Rahman, Fazlur, *Islam*, New York, Holt, Rinehart and Winston, 1967.

Rahman, Fazlur, *Islam and Modernity*, Chicago, The University of Chicago Press, 1982.

Said, Edward W., *Covering Islam*, New York, Pantheon, 1981.

——, *Orientalism*, New York, Vintage Books, Random House, 1979.

Sharif, M. Mohammed, *History of Muslim Philosophy*, 2 vols, New York, International Publications Service, 1963–66.

Sharif, Mohamed Ahmed, *Ghazali's Theory of Virtue*, Albany, State University of New York Press, 1975.

Tabataba'i, Allamah Sayyid Muhammad Husayn, *Shiite Islam*, Albany, NY, State University of New York Press, 1975.

Van Dom, Nikolas, *The Struggle for Power in Syria: Sectarianism, Regionalism and Tribalism in Politics, 1961–1978*, New York, St. Martin's Press, 1979.

Voll, John Obert, *Islam: Continuity and Change in the Modern World*, Boulder, Co., Westview Press, 1982.

Glossary

ahl al-hal wa al-'aqd: people who loose and bind; i.e. electors, the elite

ahl al-kitab: people of the book; i.e. Christians and Jews

ahl al-bayt: Prophet's family, descendants

'alim: jurist, religious scholar (pl. *ulama*)

Allah: God

Amir: ruler, prince, governor of province

Ansar: Partisans of the Prophet, i.e. the Prophet's helpers in Medina

'aql: reason

asabiyya: group solidarity

ayan: notables

bay'a: oath of allegiance to Khalife

bida: innovation

dar al-Islam: the abode of Islam

dawlah: state

din: religion

faqih: legal consultant (pl. *fuqaha*)

fardh (faridhah):   duty

fatwa: legal opinion, edict

fiqh: jurisprudence; see also *Shari'a*

fuqaha: jurists (sing. *faqih*)

ghaybah: occultation or disappearance of last Imam

hadith: saying of the Prophet

hajj: pilgrimage

hijra: the Prophet's migration to Medina

al-hukuma al-Islamiya: Islamic government

ijma: consensus

ijtihad: independent legal judgment, effort or ability to deduce rules from sources

ikhtiyar: will or freedomof will; choice

al-Ikhwan al-Muslimun: Muslim Brotherhood

'ilm: knowledge

Imam: leader of the prayers; in Shiism, spiritual leader of the *umma*:   The Institution of the Imam is known as the Imamah.
Imamiyah: the sect of Shiism
imara: governorship
infitah: 'open door' policy
ismah: in Shiism, the infallibility of the Imams
Ithna'ashari: school of Shiism that believes in a chain of twelve Imams
Jahiliyyah: period of ignorance, the pre-Islamic period of Arab history
jama'at: Islamic groups
jihad: sacred struggle
Khalafah: the institution of government legitimized by succession of the Ruler from the Prophet
khalife: successor of the Prophet; temporal leader of the *umma* in the Sunni doctrine
kharaj: tax collection
khulafa rashidun: Rightly-Guided Khalifes; the first four Khalifes
Mahdi: the Guided One; messiah
Majlis: council, parliament
Majlis al-Shura: consultative council
marja'-i taqlid: the highest mujtahid in Shiism, whose words and deeds serve as a guide for those unable to exert independent judgment
mashruta: constitutionalism
ma'sum: infallible and impeccable
mufti: one who gives *fatwa*, or legal advice
Muhajirun: those who migrated to Medina with the Prophet
mujtahid: the one who exercises his independent legal judgment; religious philosopher
mulk: dominion, kingdom
Qadhi: judge
qisas: retribution
qist: justice
qiyas: analogy
Qur'ān :   the holy book of Islam
Quraysh: the Prophet's tribe
Salaf: first three generations of Islam
Salafiyah: the movement aimed at reviving the practices and thoughts of the early generations of pious Muslims; from *salaf*, meaning the predecessors

Shahada: Muslim declaration of faith in God and the Prophethood of Muhammed

Shari'a: religious law

Shiites: followers of Ali

shura: consultation

Sufi: Islamic religious orders

sultan: ruler, king

Sunna: traditions of the Prophet

sunni: followers of the Prophet's tradition

tafsir: literal interpretation

tanzimat: reform

taqiyah: dissimulation of religious or political beliefs

taqlid: imitation of authorities in canonical matters

ta'wail: allegorical interpretation, hermeneutics

tawhid: doctrine of unity of God

tawthiq: verifying the reliability of sources

ulama: Muslim scholar, jurist

umma: community

urf: non-religious matters; customary law

wahy: revelation

waqf: Islamic endowment

wilayah: custodianship; guardianship

wizara: ministries

Zakat: alms tax

Index